MASTERING

MACMILLAN MASTER SERIES

Astronomy
Australian History
Background to Business
Banking
Basic English Law
Basic Management
Biology
British Politics
Business Communication
Business Law
Business Microcomputing
Catering Science
Chemistry
COBOL Programming
Commerce
Computer Programming
Computers
Data Processing
Economics
Electrical Engineering
Electronics
English Grammar
English Language
English Literature
Financial Accounting
French
French 2

German
Hairdressing
Italian
Italian 2
Japanese
Keyboarding
Marketing
Mathematics
Modern British History
Modern European History
Modern World History
Nutrition
Office Practice
Pascal Programming
Physics
Practical Writing
Principles of Accounts
Restuarant Service
Social Welfare
Sociology
Spanish
Spanish 2
Statistics
Statistics with your Microcomputer
Study Skills
Typewriting Skills
Word Processing

MASTERING
WORD PROCESSING

SECOND EDITION

PETER GOSLING
AND
JOANNA GOSLING

**MACMILLAN
EDUCATION**

First edition 1985
Second edition 1988

Published by
MACMILLAN EDUCATION LTD
Houndmills, Basingstoke, Hampshire RG21 2XS
and London
Companies and representatives
throughout the world

Printed in Great Britain by The Camelot Press Ltd, Southampton

British Library Catologuing in Publication Data
Gosling, P.E. (Peter Edward)
Mastering word processing.—2nd ed.
1. Word Processing systems
I. Title   II. Gosling, Joanna
652'.5
ISBN 0–333–47070–2 Pbk
ISBN 0–333–47071–0 Pbk export

CONTENTS

CONTENTS

PREFACE

Three years is a very long time in computing and many things have happened to word processing since the first edition of this book was published. The rapid decrease in the cost of the micro computer and its associated software has meant that offices who would never have dreamed of using a personal computer three years ago are now able to afford one. The wide choice of word processors available to many "ordinary" people who now have a considerable task before them when it comes to choosing the right program for the job.

The object of this new book is to probe in some depth into the funcitons that word processing package can offer and to enable new users to appreciate what is available so that they can safely choose the right program for their particular requirement – a solicitor's office will require a different range of facilities from, say, a quantity surveyor's.

This book will show you what all these options are and then compare a number of the most popular word processors now available and list their main features.

If you are thinking of buying a personal computer and word processing program then you will find this book of great use. This is because it starts you off from the beginning and is aimed not at the computer wizard but at the average secretary whose superior has realised that the use of a word processor is a Good Thing and fondly imagines, as many bosses do, that all this needed is the purchase of the machine and some software and all troubles disappear as if by magic. This is not so; it has to be worked at, and this book is designed to take the headaches out of that work.

This book was prepared using the WordPerfect word processor.l; The text was printed by an Oki laser printer and an Epson LQ1000 dot matrix printer.

The illustration used in Figure 3.18 is reproduced from Current Opinion in *Cardiology Volume 1* and is published by kind permission of Gower Academic Journals.

The photographs were by Patrick Gosling.

GLOSSARY OF COMPUTER
TRADEMARKS AND TERMS

Amstrad	(R)(TM) Amstrad Consumer Electronics Plc
CP/M	(TM) Digital Research Inc.
dBASE II	(TM) Ashton-Tate
dBASE III	(TM) Ashton-Tate
DELTA	(TM) Compsoft Plc.
DisplayWrite	(TM) IBM Corpn
Framework	(TM) Ashton-Tate
GEM	(TM) Digital Research Inc.
Hexadecimal	A hexadecimal number is a number expressed in base 16 (a decimal number is expressed in base 10); these numbers are understood by the computer to represent a character.
IBM PC	(TM) IBM Corpn
Linotronic	(TM) Allied Linotype Inc.
Locomail	(TM) Locomotive Software Ltd
Locoscript	(R)(TM) Locomotive Software Ltd
Locospell	(TM) Locomotive Software Ltd
MS-DOS	(TM) MicroSoft Corpn
MultiMate	(TM) Ashton-Tate
Advantage	(TM) Ashton-Tate
PageMaker	(TM) Aldus Corpn
PC-DOS	(TM) IBM Corpn
PCW8256	(R)(TM) Amstrad Consumer Electronics Plc
PCW8512	(R)(TM) Amstrad Consumer Electronics Plc
SuperCalc	(TM) Computer Associates
Symphony	(TM) Lotus Development Corpn
Windows	(TM) MicroSoft Corpn
WordCraft	(TM) WordCarft International
WordPerfect	(TM) WordPerfect Corpn
Wordstar	(TM) MicroPro International Corpn
WordStar 1512	(TM) MicroPro Internation Corpn

INTRODUCTION

1.1 WHAT THIS BOOK IS ABOUT

This book is an introduction to word processing and the capabilities of a number of the popular word processing systems. It is not intended to replace the comprehensive manuals supplied with each word processing program. Unfortunately some of these manuals can be rather frightening for the newcomer and so this book provides a gentle lead-in to the full story provided by the manufacturers. Manuals are very useful if you know what you are looking for and if you want to know, for example, how to deal with headers, footers, widows and orphans - always assuming you realise what these things are in the first place. This book provides an overview of typical word processing facilities and how they can help to improve and enhance the work that you process. All word processors will allow you to perform a series of basic word manipulation operations, but some will offer a number of extremely sophisticated additional functions, some of which you may need desperately and some for which you will not find any use at all.

It is often felt, by people unfamiliar with this very useful application of the new technology, that there is so much to remember and so many new things to learn, apart from the geography of the keyboard, that it offers no real advantage over the typewriter.

The keystrokes needed to perform the common word processing functions on your chosen system are usually very easy to memorise as they generally fall into a recognisable pattern. You will find that, whatever word processor you use, getting to know which key does what takes some time. You will make the most dreadful mistakes in the early stages and the whole thing will appear to be a blur until suddenly the end of the tunnel appears and you will wonder what all the fuss was about. What you will also discover is that you will rarely use all the facilities offered by the word processor you have, but at least when you do have to use one of the more obscure features you will have the confidence to try it out.

Many computer manufacturers are coming to realise that there is a great need for more "user friendliness" and so more *customised keyboards* are being produced. Not only this, but the suppliers of word processors now go out of their way to be helpful. Many of them are "menu-driven" so that you can select the operation you require in a simple manner. These make life a great deal easier for the new user. Practice, as usual, makes perfect, and remember always to read what is on the screen!

One nice thing about word processors is that your typing speed and accuracy have no bearing on the quality of the final product. The computer is very tolerant of slow typists and will never tell you to hurry up while you are looking for a particularly elusive letter on the keyboard. All the author's books are produced on a word processor and no one would flinch at the typing techniques used, except his wife who is a teacher of typing. The word processor will allow the mistakes which arise from two-fingered typing to be amended with all speed and no one is any the wiser.

1.2 INTRODUCING THE PERSONAL COMPUTER

The now very popular personal computer (PC) is a machine with a very wide range of uses, of which one is that of a word processor. It derives its versatility from the fact that it can accept information from a keyboard (very similar to that on a conventional typewriter), store it, display it on a video screen, manipulate it according to a program of instructions and then deliver it out onto a printing device. How this is actually accomplished luckily does not concern the average user at all. But like all machines one has to learn how it needs to be *treated*, what liberties can be taken with it, and just what its limitations are.

However complex such a machine is made out to be it can

never do anything that a human being cannot do. Despite
assertions to the contrary it is extremely difficult to
destroy all the information you have stored away. Not
only that, but computers do not make mistakes: people
make mistakes. Computers do as they are told quite
blindly. So if you come across a situation where someone
says, "but it has just cleared everything off the
screen!" then they must have done something to make
that happen. Computers both large and small never do
anything of their own volition.

The main parts of the modern PC are the *keyboard*, which
is your way into the machine, the *screen* and the
printer, which are its channels of communication with
the outside world, the *electronics* that perform the
manipulation of data and some form of *disk storage.*

A typical PC keyboard is shown in Figure. 1.1. You
should notice that it is just like a normal typewriter
keyboard but with a number of additions. Three of the
most important keys are the one marked **RETURN**, or **Enter**,
the one marked **Ctrl** and the one marked **Esc**. Some word
processors use the key marked **Alt** as well.

Return/Enter

This key is usually used to tell the computer that
you have *finished your instruction.* In a word
processor it is used to move the cursor - that's
the flashing line or block on the screen that
tells you where the next character is going to
appear - to the *beginning of a new paragraph.* It
is *not* the same as the Carriage Return key on an
electric typewriter. Word processors, as you will
soon see, do that for you.

Control

The Control (Ctrl) key is used in conjunction with
one or more other keys in order to produce *special
characters* or *commands.*

Escape

The Escape (Esc) key is your "panic button". If
anything goes wrong while you are using your
computer then if you press this key you can usually
stop whatever is happening.

4

Function Keys

To the left of the keyboard (or across the top in some cases) are a series of "function" keys, lettered **F1** to **F10**. These are keys used by many word processors to carry out

Fig 1.1 *PC Keyboard*

operations that otherwise would require *more than one keystroke*. The key marked **F1** is often used as a "HELP" key. Press that - or its equivalent - and you will be given help relevant to what is happening at that moment. Many help keys are said to be "context related". At the right of the keyboard is a keypad that repeats the numbers across the top of a typewriter keyboard. The 8, 2, 6 and 4 keys have arrows on them that enable you to move the cursor about the screen. This is particularly helpful while editing a document. The key marked **Home** is used by some word processors to take the cursor to the top left hand corner of the screen. The **End** key works in a similar manner taking you to the bottom of the screen. In order to use it in its alternative mode, as a numeric key pad, press the **Num Lock** key.

The electronics hidden away inside what is sometimes called the "system box" really perform two main functions. The first of these is the *electronic manipulation of data* and is performed by the now famous "microprocessor". Contrary to what you see in the press and on television, the microprocessor is not an electronic "brain". It actually operates like a telephone switchboard directing data to the appropriate parts of the machine. It also manages to perform simple arithmetic when required.

The second important part of the electronics is the memory, called **RAM** for "Random Access Memory", which operates very much like our own memory in that it can *retain a set of instructions* on how a task is to be performed together with the data to be manipulated within that task. In other words the PC's memory has to be able to retain all the word processing instructions, the program, and the text being processed.

For long term storage the PC uses *magnetic disks*, either the small removable "floppy" disks or one of these disks in conjunction with a "hard" disk. A floppy disk on most PCs will store approximately 360,000 characters (360 kilobytes: 1 keystroke = 1 character = 1 byte) and the hard disk (sometimes called a "Winchester" disk) can store anything from 10 million characters (10 Megabytes) upwards. The reason for the use of the term "floppy" and "hard" is that the former type are made of thin plastic material which is then covered with a magnetic coating and the latter type consist of rigid aluminium disks coated with a magnetic substance. Floppy disks come in a sealed square pack with a slot along a radius that allows the magnetic read and write head to fly over the surface of the disk. Under no circumstances should you touch the exposed surface of the disk. Dust and grease are death to the data on the disk. Never attempt to clean them by rubbing with a duster! Always use one of the cleaning devices recommended by your dealer.

Always insert a disk *label side upward* into the disk drive and press it gently home; then lock it into position with the locking button or lever. This is shown

in Figure 1.2. You should notice that on the left hand
side of the disk package there is a small square cut
out. This can be covered with one of the small sticky
tabs supplied with all new boxes of disks. When the cut
out is covered the computer is prevented from writing
data to the disk and is allowed only to read data from
it. The disk is then said to be "write-protected". If
the cut out is not covered then the disk can be written
to and read from.

Hard disks come in a sealed box and normally cannot be
removed from the machine. Both of them work in exactly
the same way as a domestic tape recorder - in fact these

Fig 1.2 *Inserting a disk*

were what were used for storage on the first generation
of microcomputers.

The programs you buy for your PC are always supplied on
floppy disks and you need to transfer these programs
into the memory of your PC before you can run the word
processor. This is called "loading the program". The
documents you create with your word processor are stored
on disk so that they can be recalled for future
reference when required. What you have to appreciate
before you use a word processor in practice is that
there is a difference between a "program" and the "data"
it uses. The program is a *static set of rules and
instructions* that your PC will carry out in order to

allow you to create and edit documents. The data is the text you *enter at the keyboard.*

Documents are entered initially by you at the keyboard and displayed on the screen as you proceed with your typing. Once a document is on the screen - which means that you are seeing a copy of what is stored in the RAM - you can manipulate it as you wish. You can change parts of the document, move parts of it about and delete parts of it. All this affects the data that is held in the memory. When you have completed your editing of a document you can save it away onto a magnetic disk, clear the document out of the memory and start off on the editing or preparation of another document. This might give you an inkling of one of the great advantages of using a word processor. It is that many offices have the requirement to send out letters or documents that are *basically the same each time.* Possibly the only change required is that of the date and the address. If the basic letter is stored away on a disk it can be recalled, edited and finally printed out without the need to type the whole letter each time. Many documents consist of a selection from a set of standard paragraphs strung together in different ways each time. Once those standard paragraphs have been entered and stored away they can be recalled and incorporated into a new document as many times as you wish, as you will see in Section 2.3.

1.3 PRINTERS

The final product from any word processor must be the *printed word.* There are now a variety of printing devices that can be used to produce the finished document. Until quite recently there were only two kinds of printer available. One was the "dot matrix" type where a bundle of wires are fired onto the paper through a ribbon. The pattern of wires produces the character to be printed made up of a series of dots. With early printers of this type the print quality was reasonable but not considered to be acceptable for official documents and important letters. The other was the "daisy wheel" type where the printer is more like an automatic typewriter. The characters are placed around a series of stalks fixed to a central hub and moved to the correct position above the paper before being pressed down onto a ribbon by a small hammer. The daisy wheel is removable and this enables a wide range of character styles to be used.

Recently dot matrix printers have improved rapidly in quality and many of them can now print in at least two modes; *draft mode* where the speed is around 200 characters a second and the print quality is only reasonable, and *NLQ* (Near Letter Quality) where the speed is much slower but the quality is as high as many daisy wheel printers. In addition, a dot matrix printer can be used to draw lines and boxes on your document so that you can produce your own forms if required. This is something a daisy wheel printer cannot do.

A further refinement available now is the *ink jet printer* where instead of series of pins being fired a series of jets of ink are squirted onto the paper. This has the advantage of being far quieter than either a dot matrix or a daisy wheel printer. It also produces a very high quality character due to the way that ink blob spreads slightly on the paper eliminating the dots.

The latest development in printer technology is the *laser printer*. This is a development of the photocopier and is capable of producing the highest quality text. Not only that but it is also capable of reproducing diagrams and photographs. The great use of laser printers, which are rapidly coming down in price, is in the field of Desk Top Publishing (DTP), or Second Generation Word Processors. By this technology documents of a quality equal to those produced by conventional typesetting methods can be created on an office PC.

1.4 STARTING UP YOUR PC

In order to get your PC ready to work you have to go through the procedure known as "booting it up". This is the name given to the operation of loading a special program called the "operating system" into its memory so that it is ready to *receive and run* your word processing program. Before the operating system has been loaded into memory your PC is a fairly useless chunk of electronics. The operating system breathes life into your PC in the same way that Frankenstein used the forces of Nature to breathe "life" into his monster:

there are certainly a large number of people who believe that analogy is a very close one!

If your computer has two floppy disk drives and no hard disk then you start the machine by placing a disk containing the operating system program into the drive marked **A**. If you now switch the machine on a small program stored in a ROM (Read Only Memory) inside the system box will first of all check to see if all the electronic parts of the machine are working correctly. Then it looks at the disk in drive **A** and reads the operating system into its memory. This is known as "booting the system". Now it is time for you to remove the master operating system disk and replace it with the disk containing the word processing program. The manual you get with some word processors tells you how to produce a disk that will perform the booting operation and then automatically load your word processor.

You should remember that the operating system program is a *proprietary piece of software* and it will not be supplied on the word processor disk.

If you have a hard disk system then you are saved from the task of constantly inserting and removing disks. You will be told in the word processor manual how to copy the programs onto the hard disk which already will contain the operating system program. There are various ways by which you can start your word processor from a hard disk, known as drive **C**.

Once your operating system has been loaded your PC is in a position to *accept instructions from the keyboard and carry them out*. Of course, at this stage it will only understand operating system commands. It is only when your word processing program has been loaded as well that your PC will be able to talk WordStar(R), WordPerfect(R) (see Glossary) or whatever word processor you are using.

You should note that at all times the operating system and the word processing program are *both stored in memory together*. This is because you are going to "talk" to the word processor via the keyboard, it then can communicate with the operating system to tell it to carry out certain instructions. For example, in all word processors there is a command to save a document on disk. You type this in at the keyboard and instruct WordStar, for example, to save the document. The

WordStar program then issues the instruction to the operating system to perform the saving operation. When the document has been safely saved onto a disk the operating system tells WordStar that this has been done and WordStar then informs you.

You know when the operating system is safely installed in the memory because the screen stops displaying a lot of apparently technical information (although you are often asked to type in the date and the time of day) and will display what is known as a "system prompt". This takes the form of a letter of the alphabet followed by a small arrow

A>

or

C>

On most PCs the devices containing the disks, floppy or hard, are known a "drives" and they are referred to by letters of the alphabet. If you have a PC (or a PC compatible) with two floppy disk drives then they are known as drive **A** and drive **B**. If you have a machine with a single floppy disk drive and a hard disk then the floppy disk is known as drive **A** and the hard disk is known as drive **C**. The letter displayed on the screen is that referring to the drive currently in use, the "logged disk drive". This is the drive the *operating system is looking at*. If you have a machine with twin floppy drives you can remove the DOS disk from drive **A**; it contains the master operating system program that has now been copied into memory. This disk should always be kept in a safe place, for without it your PC cannot be started up. Now you can replace this disk with one that contains the word processing program and load that into memory as well. *Then you are ready to start word processing.*

If you have a PC with a hard disk drive then, because its capacity is far greater than a floppy disk, your word processing program can be already installed on it ready to go. General instructions for the starting of word processing programs will be detailed a little later (Section 1.7).

1.5 LOOKING AT THE OPERATING SYSTEM

Once your operating system program has been safely
loaded into memory there are a number of things it can
do for you either before or after you have used a word
processor. The operating system, usually called MS-DOS
(MicroSoft Disk Operating System) or PC-DOS (see
Glossary), contains a set of programs often known as
"utilities" that help you to *organise your PC
efficiently*. Although a lot of these are of use only to
the computer scientist a number of them can be of great
value to the word processor operator. A short
description of these now follows. Each of these programs
is set into motion by typing the name given in word
processor type. Take note of the layout of each command
and make sure that it is copied exactly. The position of
the *spaces* is critical. You must make sure that you type
the command as it is given to you and not what you think
it ought to be! End every command by pressing the
RETURN/ENTER) key. This is the key that says, "Over to
you".

> **DIR** This is the program that gives a list of *every
> file stored on a specified disk* It will list the
> name of the file, the number of bytes (characters)
> it contains, its date of creation and the time of
> creation. In addition it will tell you how much
> *space* is left on the disk.
>
> A>**DIR** This will list all the files on the disk in
> drive **A** as shown in Figure 1.3.

Fig 1.3 *Listing the files on a disk*

WP9JO	BK!	57268	5-02-88	15:09
JO	DOC	98	13-12-87	21:05
JOTEST	DOC	98	7-02-88	22:10
WP9JO		63266	5-02-88	13:45
PAGINATE		1475	1-03-88	15:51
WP3		25567	3-03-88	9:12

         19 File(s)   126976 bytes free

A>**DIR B:** This will list all the files on the disk in drive **B**.

A>**DIR/P** This will display the *file list*, but *a page at a time*. This is because it is possible that there may be so many files on the disk that their names will occupy more than the twenty four lines of the screen. This amendment to the command will allow you to read the file list at your leisure.

You will probably notice that most file names are followed by a three-letter "extension". This extension tells us something about the type of file it is. A file name followed by **DOC** or **TXT** would be a document or a text file, one followed by **EXE** or **COM** are *program* files. File names can consist of a combination of no more than eight letters and numbers. A complete file name will consist of three parts: the drive on which it is currently located, its name and its extension. The drive name is separated from the name by a colon,:, and the file name is separated from the extension by a fullstop.(period). Hence the name

A:JBLET1.DOC

refers to a file called **JBLET1** on the disk in drive **A** which has a **DOC** extension (sometimes referred to as a "dot DOC" extension), telling us that it is a *document*. If there is no drive name prefixing the file name it is assumed to be on the logged disk drive.

You can use "wild cards" in file names. These are the characters **?** and *****. By using wild card characters you can list, for example, all the document files on the disk in drive **A** by the command

A>DIR *.DOC

as shown in Figure 1.4.

Fig 1.4 *Listing all the document files on a disk*

                 Directory of A:

        BSLETT1   DOC   198   12-11-87   12:35
        JOTEST1   DOC   98   18-01-88   11:07
        JO   DOC   98   13-12-87   21:05
        JOTEST   DOC   98   7-02-88   22:10

           4 File(s)   **126976 bytes free**

All the files on drive **B** that start with the letters TH are listed by the command

A>**DIR B :TH*.***

If you want to list all the files that are five characters long and can have anything in the first three places but must have the number 86 following them you can use the command

A>**DIR ???86.***

The **?** character stands for a single character, but ***** stands for any number of characters. This system of wild cards is also used in the **COPY** and **DEL** instructions that are detailed later in this section.

FORMAT This will allow you to prepare a *blank floppy disk* to *receive saved documents*. If you have a twin floppy disk machine the instruction is issued with the master operating system disk in drive **A** and a blank disk in drive **B**. The instruction is then

A>**FORMAT B:**

Formatting a disk will wipe everything off the disk if you happen to have a used disk in drive B. This is perfectly all right if you have nothing on the disk you wish to keep. It enables you to re-use disks containing out-of-date documents. Whatever you do, do not - unless you really are aware of the consequences - issue the command without a specified drive name after the word **FORMAT**. DOS will always assume that the *current drive* is meant if no drive name is specified. This could result in you reformatting the DOS disk. Not something you normally would wish to do!

COPY This allows you to take a *copy of a file* and *place it on another disk*.

A>COPY JBLET1.DOC B:

will place a copy of the file called **LETTER1.DOC** on the disk in drive **A** onto the disk in drive **B**.

A>COPY JBLET1.DOC B:JBLET2.DOC

will place a copy of the file called **JBLET1.DOC** on the disk in drive **A** onto the disk in drive **B**, but this time the copy will be called **JBLET2.DOC**. The instruction to copy a set of files from one disk to another could look like this

A>COPY *.DOC B :

which would all the files with a **DOC** extension on the disk in drive **A** onto the disk in drive **B**.

DISKCOPY This command will allow you to make an identical copy of one floppy disk onto another. **DISKCOPY** formats the "target" disk before copying takes place. The command looks like this

A>DISKCOPY A : B :

which tells the operating system to make a copy of the disk in drive **A** onto the disk in drive **B**. The way to do it is ensure that the operating system disk is in drive **A** before issuing the command. You will then be told to place the "source" disk in drive A and the "target" disk in drive **B**. This means that you have to remove the master operating system disk and then replace it with the disk to be copied.

DEL This command will *erase* a file from a disk. Once deleted a file *cannot normally be recovered.* In order to delete, for example, all the files from the disk in drive **A** that have **BAK** extensions - **BAK** files are backup files and are the copies made by WordStar of a document before it has been edited; this means that it is the previous version to the one now saved under the original name - you tell the operating system

A>**DEL *.BAK**

This will delete all **BAK** files from drive **A** and

A>**DEL B:*.BAK**

will delete all **BAK** files from the disk in drive **B**. Beware, unless you really mean to do it, of the command

A>**DEL *.***

Luckily the operating system will query you by asking

Are you Sure? (Y/N)

since this command will *delete every file on the disk irrespective of its name and extension.*

1.6 **KEEPING TRACK OF FILES**

This section applies particularly to those users who have a PC with a hard disk drive. Hard disk drives can store several hundred files, but by virtue of this - and our natural reluctance to get rid of anything if we do not really need to - it becomes quite a task to keep track of what we have got. Two golden rules are:

1. Keep program files and document files *separate from each other.*

2. Devise a *naming system* so that you can identify a file from its name.

The first rule is fairly easy to apply if you have a twin floppy disk system. It is to keep the program disk in drive **A**; this is usually not difficult to do as most systems force you to do it. Additionally you should make sure that you *never store* any documents on this disk. Always ensure that documents are saved on the disk currently in drive **B**. This then makes it easy to store the documents in groups by allocating specific disks to particular types of documents.

If you have a hard disk system you can approach the problem in several ways. It relies on the fact that you divide the disk up into a series of *sub-directories*. This splits the storage areas up into parts, one of which can be allocated to a word processing program, another part to an accounting program, another to a financial modelling program and so on. If your disk has no sub-directories every time you issue the command

C>**DIR**

you will get a list of files stored in the "root", or main, directory. However, you can organise your disk in a *tree-like structure* so that leading from this root are a series of "branches" as shown in Figure 1.5.

Fig 1.5 *Directory organisation : a tree with its "branches"*

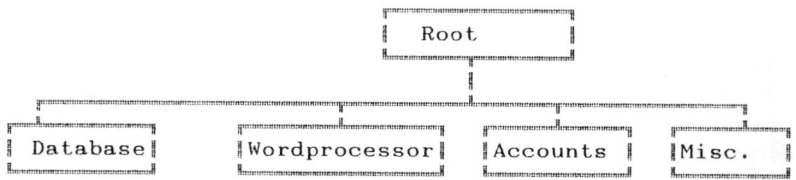

In order to create a sub-directory the command **MD** or **MKDIR** (Make Directory) is used

C>MD WP

In order to get into that part of the disk now you have to use the command **CD** or **CHDIR**, (Change Directory)

C>CD \WP

and you will be moved into the new directory, which, if you use the **DIR** command now will be seen to be *empty*. Note the \ backslash character, that *separates the command from the name of the sub-directory*.

In order to return to the root directory all you need is the command

C>CD

It is very easy to copy files into this directory from a floppy disk by going into the directory, using **CD \WP**, and then using the command

C>COPY A:*.*

This will then copy all the files from the floppy disk in drive **A** into that sub-directory. Alternatively, the word processor manual supplied with your software may tell you exactly how to set up the program to run from a hard disk.

Every time you wish to use the word processor you can enter that directory and ensure that all the documents you create and edit are kept on a disk in the floppy disk drive. Alternatively, if your word processor allows you to do so, you could keep your documents in yet another sub-directory on your hard disk well out of the way of accounts files and other irrelevant material.

Try always to use names *relevant to the documents you are saving*. To name them as **LETTER1, LETTER2,** etc. makes it very difficult to identify the recipient of any letter. If you use a more meaningful naming system you will have a better chance of keeping track of everything. For example, remembering that you have *eight* characters available for every file name, you could reserve the first three for a company identifier, the second two for a type code and the last three for a serial number. This would mean that a file called **DFRLT004** would refer to the fourth letter to a company called "D.F.Robinson" and **HJTQT016** would be the sixteenth quotation to "H.J.Taylor". So long as the system is consistent and simple, you will have few problems.

1.7 **INSTALLING A WORD PROCESSOR**

When you receive your word processing program it will arrive smartly wrapped in plastic and will consist of a bulky manual and one or more disks. With the disks will come a *licence agreement* which you should sign and return to the supplier. It will usually consist of an agreement by which you will undertake not to copy the program for use on more than one machine, and certainly not for passing on to your friends. It also usually ensures that any amendments to the program will be supplied to you in the event of there being some "bug" in the program that stops it performing certain tasks under certain conditions. In addition this licence agreement will often allow you to purchase an *upgrade to the program* at preferential rates when the suppliers bring out an improved version, as they are almost sure to do.

The passing on of "pirate" versions of commercial programs has been a thorn in the side of many suppliers of software and recent court cases have indicated that the law can be ruthless with anyone found passing illicit copies around, especially for money. You are warned never to have anything to do with anyone who offers you software of any sort, not just word processors, with manuals that are photocopies and disks that have handwritten labels without a manufacturer's serial number.

Once you have opened the package look in the printed material for instructions on what to do first of all. This will usually consist of a set of operations that you will have to perform in order to make copies of the disks supplied. This is done by using the operating system **FORMAT** and **COPY** or **DISKCOPY** commands as described in Section 1.5 of this chapter, particularly if you have a twin floppy disk machine. If you have a hard disk machine you will probably be told to create a sub-directory and copy the contents of the disks into that. Whichever type of machine you have you should arrange that the original disks are used once only and that copies are used in the everyday running of your word processor. The reason for this is that if by any chance any damage is done to one of the original disks you will probably have to purchase a completely new set. If you have not carried out the supplier's instructions then you will get little sympathy.

Once you have made copies of the master word processing disks you are in a position to begin the *installation* of your word processing program. Store the master disks away in a safe place. Hopefully, you will never have to use them again. Then read the instructions for the installation of your word processor. The installation routine is very important because it allows you to customise the program to work on your particular machine. Even with the proliferation of IBM PC "clones" there are often slight differences between them. It is particularly important to make sure that the *screen display is correct* and your *printer works properly*. The installation program is usually called **INSTALL** - check this with your manual, and follow its instructions carefully and to the letter. If by any chance something goes wrong you can exit from the program; it will tell you how to do this. Then you can start again. But make sure you read the screen display carefully as you proceed with each step.

The screen display is important to get right because many word processors will show underlining and bold face type on the screen when you have issued the appropriate command to the word processor.

It is of paramount importance to make sure that the word processor knows exactly *which printer is connected* so that full use is made of the facilities it offers.

There are over 250 different printers available at the present time and they are not all by any means identical. Apart from the differences in manufacturer there are various types and sub-types you may have to make allowances for.

Ignoring for the moment that there are several different ways of transferring characters onto paper there are two basic ways for your machine to *communicate with a printer*. These are "serial" and "parallel". The serial socket will sometimes be known as "**the RS 232 port**" and may be labelled as such.

Bear in mind that the printer obtains its instructions by a series of electrical pulses sent down the wires connecting it to the computer; it is this pattern of pulses that tell it to print a letter "A" or a letter "a" and to print it in bold, **A** or **a,** or underlined, <u>A</u> or <u>a</u>, or underlined and bold, **<u>A</u>** or **<u>a</u>**. Codes can even be sent to print characters oversize or undersize, superscripted or subscripted. Most word processors are "wysiwyg" which is short for "what you see is what you get". This means that what you see on the screen will give you a *good idea of what the finished product will look like*.

In simple terms, the instructions to a printer come in *sets of eight* and they can be sent to the printer in one of two ways appropriate to the design of the printer. A "serial" printer expects the pulses to be sent "serially" to it, which means that the eight pulses are sent *one after the other* along a pair or wires. A "parallel" printer expects all eight to be sent *simultaneously* along a set of eight parallel wires. A piece of electronics inside the printer then decodes these pulses and arranges for the correct character to be printed. In fact, each printer contains a small computer in order to handle this operation.

If you have purchased a serial printer then it must be plugged into the socket at the back of your computer marked "**SERIAL**" or "**SERIAL PORT**". A parallel printer must be plugged into the "**PARALLEL**" socket.

The most popular types of printer are of the parallel type, but you should check just to make sure, because when the installation routine is running you should be ready to answer the question "Is it a parallel or serial printer?" correctly.

Most word processors can handle the various types of printer and you will usually have a list displayed from which you can tell the program the make and type of printer you have. This usually takes care of the daisy wheel/dot matrix choice. Laser printers are usually dealt with in a separate section.

Not only can you specify the type of printer but you can also arrange for the word processor to know that it prints on continuous stationery, single sheets or a cut sheet feeder. Many people use high quality continuous stationery with perforations that can be torn off leaving a clean edge. Such stationery can be pre-printed for you if required and this allied with 'micro perforations" make the final result indistinguishable from single sheets. The output is faster than that from single sheets fed through automatically. Attachments can be put on most printers to give you the option of single sheet (hand fed), continuous stationery and automatic sheet feed. These are shown in Figures 1.6, 1.7 and 1.8.

There are some word processors that allow you to configure for *more than one printer*. This enables you to have a situation where you have one printer that is fast, but not such high quality, for draft copies of documents and another that is of high quality for the finished article. Your computer can be connected to two printers at once by means of a switch box, the switch at the front allowing you to select the printer you require. One of these is shown in Figure 1.9. Alternatively, if you have a printer that can run in more than one mode, draft or NLQ then you can set it up so as to appear to the word processor that you have two printers and let the software take over when you select the printer you require.

Fig 1.6 *Single sheet feed*

Fig 1.7 *Continuous stationery*

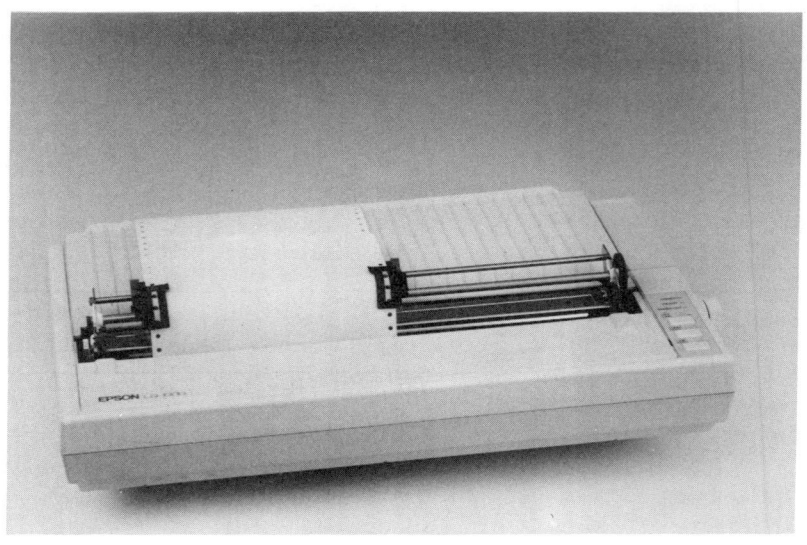

Fig 1.8 *Automatic sheet feed*

Fig 1.9 *Switch box*

SUMMARY

1. Your *PC* consists of a screen, a keyboard, a system box and a printer.
2. The *system box* contains the computer, the memory and either two floppy disk drives or a hard disk and a single floppy disk.
3. *Floppy disks* are removable but store far fewer documents than hard disks. The disks are used for long term storage of documents.
4. The important *keys* on the keyboard are **Ctrl**, **Alt**, **Return/Enter** and **Esc**. Many word processors use the ten **F** (Function) keys as well.
5. Load the operating system into the computer's memory *before* loading the word processing program.

6. Always make a *copy of the master disks* supplied for your word processor.

7. Use the copies to *instal* the system and for *day-to-day running*.

8. Follow the *supplier's instructions* in order to install your word processor correctly so that it can use your equipment - particularly the printer-efficiently.

9. You can often configure your word processor to use *more than one type of printer*.

10. *Printers* can be dot matrix, for fast medium quality or slow high quality printing, daisy wheel for high quality printing and laser printers for very high quality printing with the ability to reproduce pictures and diagrams.

11. The important *operating system commands* are **DIR**, **COPY**, **DISKCOPY**, **MD**, **CD**, **FORMAT** and **DEL**.

12. *Files* can have names made from up to eight characters and an optional three character extension.

13. For economy of space divide your hard disk up into a series of *sub-directories*.

14. Always keep document files and program files on disks in *different drives* or in *different directories*.

BASIC WORD

PROCESSING

2.1 CREATING A DOCUMENT

In order to start your word processor going so that you can create a document you will have to make sure that the correct *start-up disk* is in drive **A**, if you have a twin floppy disk machine. If you have a hard disk machine check that you are in the correct *directory*. Make sure that you have found the command to *start the program working* from the manufacturer's manual. It is usually a simple command word or sequence of letters that relate to the name of word processor. For example

A>**WS**

will start WordStar and

A>**WP**

will start WordPerfect. Usually the next thing to happen is that you are presented with some sort of *opening menu* from which you choose what you want to do. An opening menu will give you a set of options including such things as

1. Create a new document.
2. Edit an existing document.
3. Print a document.

If you want help to explain some aspect of the menu then there is usually a **HELP** facility available. Select the option to create a new document and watch what happens. Follow any instructions that may be displayed. You will be presented with what is basically a blank sheet of paper upon which you can type whatever you wish. You will see that you are always told the *current cursor* position in terms of the column number, line number and page number on what is called the "status line" or "scale line". This is usually displayed across the top of the screen. A ruler line, or "format line", across the top of the screen is often displayed as well as a status line giving you the *current width* of your document and the position of the tab stops. These are set by default by the program and can always be changed by you at any time. The term "default" is used to refer to settings of such things as margins and tabs that are put into the ruler line by the program when you start it up. Another common default setting is, strangely enough, to make the document drive - that is the disk drive where documents are stored - be drive **A**. This accounts for the lowest common denominator of PCs to be used, those with a single disk drive only. Default settings can usually be *altered by you*.

All you need to do now is to *begin typing*. As you do so you will find that there is no need to perform a carriage return at the end of each line as you do with a conventional typewriter. Word processors provide what is called "word wrap" which means that when a word spills over to the right of the right hand margin the program will automatically provide a carriage return and line feed to bring you to the beginning of the next line. The only time you need to press the **RETURN** key in a document is when you get to the end of a paragraph and you want to insert what is known as a "hard return". You will also do this when you want to insert a *blank line* in your document.

As you type you may want to underline certain characters, or have them printed in bold type. In order to do this you have to issue certain commands that differ from word processor to word processor but embed in the text an instruction to the printer to switch the function on. When you have reached the end of the section you have underlined or emboldened, or both, you have to *switch the command off*. This usually involves the same command as is used to switch the function on. A command used in this way is known as a "toggle". If you want to indent the first word of a paragraph by a certain number of characters then you press the **TAB** key which will move the cursor to the first tab stop position. Again, this embeds a code in the text telling the printer to move to that tab position before commencing to print that line.

Word processors tend to be set up around the A4 size of page and so a page length of 66 lines is the standard in use. You can change this in case you still have a stock of foolscap paper or want to print on smaller sheets or labels. At the end of each page you will usually see a line drawn across the screen by the program to tell you that you have reached the end of a page and are about to start another. You should notice that the actual number of lines printed on a page is usually 54 to allow for margins at the top and bottom. This number can be altered by you if you wish. You can, however, force a new page before the true bottom of the page has been reached by inserting a code into the text that tells the printer to "throw a new page". Figure 2.1, using a dummy word processor, shows how this operates. First of all we show what the text looks like on the screen. The ruler line is along the top; **L** and **R** show the left and right margins and the \ character indicates a tab position.

Fig 2.1 *A memorandum on the screen*

```
L-----|-----|-----|-----|-----|-----|-----|-----|-----|-----|-----R
              MEMORANDUM

     To: All Heads of Department        21/9/87

     From: Financial Director

     A short meeting is to be held in my office on
     Friday 25th October at 9.30 a.m.

     The sales figures for the past three months have
     fallen below our forecasts and urgent steps will
     have to be made to improve these in the future.
     This meeting is to investigate ways in which this
     can be implemented.

     J.T.Robinson
```

If the text can be examined - and many word processors allow you to do this - you will see that hidden away inside the text are certain codes: **[B]** for embolden, **[TAB]** for tabs, **[HRT]** for a hard return, **[SRT]** for a "soft" return that is put in by the word processor in order to wrap the next word onto the next line because there is no more space left for it on the current line. The actual stored text looks as shown in Figure 2.2

Fig 2.2 *A memorandum : stored text with "hidden" codes*

[TAB][TAB][B]MEMORANDUM[B][HRT]
[HRT]
To: All Heads of Department[TAB][TAB]21/9/87[HRT]
[HRT]
From: Financial Director[HRT]
[HRT]
A short meeting is to be held in my office on[SRT]
Friday 25th October at 9.30 a.m.[HRT]
[HRT]
The sales figures for the past three months have[SRT]
fallen below our forecasts and urgent steps will[SRT]

All the codes, with the exception of the soft returns put in by the word processor are entered by the operator. Your job as a word processor user is to learn *how to produce these codes* for the particular word processor you are using.

There are, of course, many more of these codes that are provided by a word processor, you will find that you soon become used to using them.

2.2 SAVING AND PRINTING

Once you have created your document you will need to do at least one of three things. You may want to *save* the document away for future use, *print* it out or *abandon* it.

If you want to save the document then you have to decide on a *name to call it*, depending on your naming convention, since it *cannot be saved if it has no name*. Very often you will have had to name the document before you even start to create it, in which case you just issue the command to save the current document and it will be saved on disk.

There are a number of options available to you when you save a document. You are usually able to choose between:

1. *Saving the document and continuing with editing.* This enables you to keep a copy of a document against the possibility of a system failure. In such a situation you will not then lose all your work.

2. Saving the document and returning to the point where you are *ready to edit or create another.*

3. Saving the document and *leaving the word processor.*

4. Saving the document and *printing it immediately.*

5. Leaving the document without saving it. This you would do if you made so many errors that you decided that it was better to start all over again.

What you have to make sure of is that the document will be saved *where you want it to be saved.* This would be on the disk in drive **B** if you have a floppy disk system, or in a particular sub-directory if you have a hard disk system. So make sure you know how to *specify such things.* Your manual will tell you.

Most word processors make you *save a document before you can print it.* This means that you have to save the document first, as mentioned above, and then the program has to be instructed to print the saved program. There are several word processors, however, that allow printing directly from memory without having to save the document first. This is a time-saving process - and a space-saving process as well since it can often happen that you may not want to keep a copy of the document (the memorandum shown in Figure 2.1 for example) on disk for future use. If you do not save the document then it is lost as soon as you either switch off the machine or start a new document.

A useful feature, similar to that just described, is

that it is often possible to use your word processor in *typewriter mode*. You can either arrange for it to print each character as you press the key or to allow you to enter a line of text, edit it if you wish, and then print it out. In this case you are using the word processor as an editing typewriter producing one line of type at a time. This is very useful if you are going to have to produce *addresses on envelopes*.

Addresses on envelopes are notoriously difficult to produce on a printer. This is because of the thickness of the envelope being printed on. There are two alternatives. If you have a lot of names and addresses to type you can buy envelopes connected together as continuous stationery. They can then be fed through the printer by the tractor feed mechanism used for continuous stationery. They can then be taken off the printer, separated and the perforations stripped off to produce the separate envelopes. An alternative is for you to use peel-off sticky labels and use the word processor in typewriter mode to print individual names and addresses. This is also a useful method if you are doing a mailshot (which will be described in detail later) and want to print several hundred labels. Another alternative is to use window envelopes.

When you print a document you often have a number of choices available to you regarding the way that the *printing is performed*. You can, if you have a multipaged document, chose to print selected pages only or you can choose to print several copies of the same document in one operation. In many word processors it is at the time of printing that you have the choice of printer given to you, as mentioned in Section 2.1.

2.3 EDITING A DOCUMENT

If you have a document saved away on disk and you want to amend it in some way then your first task is to *retrieve* it from its disk and *display* it on the screen. When you do this you will always get the beginning of the document displayed. You are likely then to have to *search through* the document to find the part you wish to edit. Each word processor has its own individual command for allowing you to move through a document, but they all allow you to move in *steps of varying sizes*. You can usually move through a document character by character, word by word, paragraph by paragraph or page by page. You often will have the facility to move directly to the top or bottom of the current page. These commands will all be similar and usually use the *arrow keys* on the keypad at the right of the keyboard.

Once you have reached the point where you want to start editing you can delete characters, words or whole blocks of text if you want. The first two of these - and sometimes the deletion of a complete paragraph - are accomplished usually with a command that is similar to the one that moves you by one word or paragraph. Deletion of one character is dealt with by the key marked **Del**. The screen can be set up to be in **Insert** or **Overtype** mode, (the names depend on the word processor in use). If you are in the first of these you will see that whatever you type in the body of a document is fitted in automatically as the characters to the right move over to allow space for the extra characters. If you select the second mode you are using the word processor as a conventional typewriter and you type over the existing characters replacing them with different ones.

In editing a document you can add and remove the embedded codes for underlining, emboldening and other features. They can be treated just like any other characters in the text.

If you wish, you can move text around very easily so that it is possible to change the *order of paragraphs* without having to retype any of them. A very simple test that you should be able to perform when you have had some practice with a word processor is to take the lines of the rhyme in Figure 2.3a, that are out of order

Fig 2.3a *A disorganised rhyme*

5 This little piggy went "ee, ee" all the way home
2 This little piggy stayed at home
1 This little piggy went to market
4 This little piggy had none
3 This little piggy ate roast beef

and rearrange them to become the rhyme in Figure 2.3b.

Fig 2.3b *A reorganised rhyme*

```
1 This little piggy went to market
2 This little piggy stayed at home
3 This little piggy ate roast beef
4 This little piggy had none
5 This little piggy went "ee, ee" all the way home
```

Editing can also involve *searching* for a particular set of characters in order to go to a specified part of the document. All word processors have this facility and it involves specifying exactly what string of characters is being searched for and setting the word processor off to find them. It does this by attempting to match the characters you are looking for with each group of the same number of characters in the document. When it finds a match, then the search stops. An extension of this is to *search and replace*. In this case you can search throughout your document for the required characters. Each time they are found they are exchanged for some other set of characters. For example in the piece of text in Figure 2.4a it might be required to change every occurrence of the word "Norfield" into the word "Strangtown".

Fig 2.4a *A voting address : the MP for Norfield*

I should like to take this opportunity to
state to the voters of Norfield that I
intend to serve them to the best of my
ability. I have long regarded Norfield as a
place where the voters are intelligent and
discerning, which is more than can be said
for some areas of the country. As I have
said, Norfield is a place I long to serve
and it is my intention to make my home here
in Norfield as soon as you have had the good
sense to give me the votes I am sure I
deserve.

The result is that the final text becomes that in Figure 2.4b.

Fig 2.4b *Voting address : after defeat and re-election*

I should like to take this opportunity to
state to the voters of Strangtown that I
intend to serve them to the best of my
ability. I have long regarded Strangtown as
a place where the voters are intelligent and
discerning, which is more than can be said
for some areas of the country. As I have
said, Strangtown is a place I long to serve
and it is my intention to make my home here
in Strangtown as soon as you have had the
good sense to give me the votes I am sure I
deserve.

You should notice that the lengths of the lines have
been adjusted automatically by the program to take
account of the fact that the replacement word is *longer*
than the original. Not all word processors do this
automatically for you but those that do not will allow
you to reform the paragraph so that it looks neat and
tidy.
Another form of editing is that where *additional text*
is brought into the document *from outside*. For example,
if there were several alternative paragraphs available
for insertion into a letter they could each be saved
away in files called, say, **PARA1**, **PARA2** and **PARA3**.An
outline letter could be stored that can have the
appropriate paragraph entered into it. The standard
letter might be as in Figure 2.5.

Fig 2.5 *A standard letter*

> DATE
>
> NAME
> ADDRESS1
> ADDRESS1
> ADDRESS3
>
> Dear NAME
>
> Thank you for your enquiry for a credit account.
>
> Yours faithfully
>
> J.K.Upex
>
> Credit Manager

PARA1 might be

> **We are sorry that we are unable to open a credit account for you.**

PARA2 might be

> **We are glad to offer you a credit account and are glad that you have decided to give us the benefit of your valued custom.**

and **PARA3** might be

> **We will be glad to offer you the service of a credit account on receipt of references from two local retailers with whom you have had a similar account over the past three years.**

The final letter might first of all look like Figure 2.6.

Fig 2.6 *Final letter with inserted text*

> DATE
>
> NAME
> ADDRESS1
> ADDRESS1
> ADDRESS3
>
> Dear NAME
>
> Thank you for your enquiry for a credit account.
>
> We are sorry that we are unable to open a credit account for you.
>
> Yours faithfully
>
> J.K.Upex
>
> Credit Manager

where **PARA1** has been inserted in the letter. It only remains now to use **Overtype** mode to change the date, name and address lines (Figure 2.7).

Fig 2.7 *Final addressed letter*

> 25th October 1987
>
> Mr J.Harris
> 21 High Street
> Norfield
> Blankshire
>
> Dear Mr Harris
>
> Thank you for your enquiry for a credit account.
>
> We are sorry that we are unable to open a credit account for you.
>
> Yours faithfully
>
> J.K.Upex
>
> Credit Manager

SUMMARY

1. When creating a document press the **RETURN** key *only* when you reach the *end of a paragraph.*
2. Use the **tab key** to indent the *first word of a paragraph.*
3. All *control commands* (bold, underline, etc.) are embedded in the text and can be deleted whenever required.
4. Whenever you have to produce letters following a *standard format* save frequently repeated paragraphs on disk and call them into the letters whenever they are required.
5. You can always *search* for a particular word and replace it with another without a laborious manual search through the whole document.

COMING TO TERMS

This chapter explains and illustrates a number of the terms used and the facilities offered by word processors. Not all word processors offer all these facilities, but most of them will give you a good selection of what follows.

3.1 JUSTIFICATION

When a conventional mechanical typewriter is being used the typist has control over the appearance of the *right-hand* end of each line of type. Decisions can be made as to whether the last word of the line is to be hyphenated or a space left at the end of the line with the word typed at the start of the next line. The result is a "ragged" right hand margin. If a piece of text in a book or a newspaper is set by hand (not a very common practice these days) the compositor or typesetter is able to insert small extra spaces between the words in order to provide a clean right-hand margin. This operation produces what is called "right justified text". It is a very skilled operation and is possible on a typewriter only if the number of letters in each line is counted and the typist puts the spaces in as each line is typed. The final result takes a lot of time, but the appearance of the finished text is very much enhanced.

With a word processor we can leave the task of *counting the letters and words* and *inserting the correct number of spaces* to the program if required. The problem is however, not as simple as that. Compare the two identical pieces of text shown in Figures 3.1 and 3.2. The first of these shows the text printed with no justification and the second shows it right justified. Notice particularly the unsightly extra spaces in the first line of Figure 3.2. These are there because the program knows how many characters there are to be in a line and that the first word on the second line is too long to be included in the line above and so the spaces left over - there has to be at least one between each word - are inserted reasonably evenly between the ten words on that line. You might also notice that the words themselves can look strange because each letter is allowed to take up the same character width. But an "i" is not as wide as, for example, an "r" or an "f", so if you look at the word "frightened" on the second line you will see that the word takes up rather too much space and this is particularly noticeable when the text is justified. These irritations can be resolved as you will see in Sections 3.5 and 3.10.

A special form of right-hand justification is when you wish to have a document where (although it is not justified in the sense described above) you need to have a clean right-hand edge and a clean left-hand edge as well. An example of this is a theatre programme as is shown in Figure 3.3. One way you can do this is by using *decimal tabs*, which are covered in Section 3.2 below.

3.2 TABS AND INDENTS

Laying out documents clearly has always been an essential part of secretarial training and one important part of this is setting tabs and margins. Tabs (short for "tabulator" stops) are places along the ruler line that you can move to quickly by pressing the **TAB** key in order to make sure that, for example, all paragraphs start in the same place or that lists are always lined up vertically. Margins define the left- and right-hand edges of your text and the tab stops fall within the left- and right-hand margins.

Very often you may want to have a part of your text with shorter lines that the rest so that it is *inset* within the main text. See Figure 3.1.

Fig 3.1 *Text with no justification*

In a letter to a woman's magazine recently a reader
wrote that she was frightened of computers and that

> I was told by a computer addict that my
> plans for becoming an interpreter were
> pointless. He said that wordprocessors
> would soon replace the human....

First of all I should like to reassure the lady that her
fears are quite groundless. One can gauge the quality
of the advice given by the adviser being described as a
'computer addict'. These so-called experts are among
the worst advocates of the new technology and are prone
to cloud the real issues with mythology and mumbo-jumbo.
No wonder the average adult person is terrified of
anything to do with computers. Of course, the popular
press and television do not help a lot either. The
advice the reader has been given was unfortunately
typical of wrong thinking by the so-called computer
enthusiasts who have a very narrow and highly coloured
view of what computers can and cannot do.

Fig 3.2 *Text with right justification*

In a letter to a woman's magazine recently a reader
wrote that she was frightened of computers and that

> I was told by a computer   addict that my
> plans for   becoming an interpreter were
> pointless. He said   that wordprocessors
> would soon replace the human....

First of all I should like to reassure the lady that her
fears are quite groundless. One can gauge the quality
of the   advice given by the adviser being described as a
'computer addict'. These so-called   experts are among
the worst   advocates of the new technology and are prone
to cloud the real issues with mythology and mumbo-jumbo.
No wonder the average adult   person is terrified of
anything to do with computers. Of course, the popular
press and television do not help a lot either. The
advice the   reader has been given was unfortunately
typical of   wrong thinking by the so-called computer
enthusiasts who have a very narrow and highly coloured
view of what computers can and cannot do.

Many documents have to contain *figures*, and it has always been the bane of a typist's life to have to make sure that all the numerals line up in a sensible manner. In the same way that ordinary tabs are set up - so that when the tab key is pressed the cursor hops to the next tab stop so that the first character you type appears in the correct column - you can arrange for all the *decimal points* to be set up under each other. Whenever you set up tabs on a word processor you are given the choice of setting them up as decimal tabs if required. The program will tell you what key to press if you want to set a "**dec tab**". The result is that when you tab to the chosen position you find the that as you enter a number the figures move from right to left instead of left to right as in conventional typing. When you press the decimal point key (the full-stop key) entry proceeds as normal. The result is shown in Figure 3.4.

Very often you can use a decimal tab to achieve the result shown in Figure 3.3 where the right hand column of names is aligned on the last letter, producing a clean right edge. The clean left edge is, of course, produced from a conventional tab stop.

Fig 3.3 *A justified theatre programme using* **dec. tab**

CAST LIST

Sir Roger Frampton	Charles Jones
Lady Eleanor	Julia Walker
The Hon. Freddy	Raymond Wilkes
Mrs Drudge	Amelia Fairburn
Jean Francis	Heather Frazer
Johnnie Francis	Jim Hall
Inspector Gregory	Alistair Watts
H.Z.Bloomstein	Harry Saunders
A Stranger	Bill Walker

Fig 3.4 *Using* **dec. tab**

```
     5
    56
   563
  5634.
  5634.5
  5634.57
```

3.3 PAGINATION

Pagination (or repagination, as it is sometimes called) helps you to sort out your pages. When you are working on a long document you may end up having to move large pieces of text around, delete paragraphs, or pages, and the end result can be disappointing. Without pagination a document could print out with pages of different lengths.

Some programs, such as WordPerfect, do not need a pagination program because all the system page ends move automatically as text is amended. Text is reformed to fit between margins and footnotes renumbered automatically. Not all programs do this. However, even WordPerfect is not clever enough to decide which of the page breaks you set manually are still viable and which are not.

A *pagination command* will sort out your document. You can set the ideal number of lines you would like to keep on a page and then run the program. Some word processors ask you whether "widows" and "orphans" are acceptable during pagination; these terms will be explained in Section 3.4. Others want to know whether to adjust line endings and reform text at the same time. The Display-Write series will repaginate your document while it is being checked for spelling mistakes, which kills two birds with one stone.

If you do not want paragraphs to be split up when the document is reorganised you may need to use a "keep lines together" command which will keep a specified number of lines together on one page and will take the whole lot over onto the next page rather than split them.

3.4 **WIDOWS AND ORPHANS**

"Widows" and "orphans" are printing terms that refer to the situations where the first line of a new paragraph is printed all on its own at the bottom of a page or the last line - or, worse still, the last word, of a paragraph - is printed on its own at the top of a page. The situation is shown in Figures 3.5 and 3.6. In the first of these the line at the top of Page 2 is an "orphan" and upsets the look of that page. Figure 3.6 shows the result of telling the word processor that it must protect widows and orphans, which it has done by transferring the last line of Page 1 onto the first line of Page 2. This, of course, reduces the number of lines on the first page by one, but it is not noticeable.

3.5 **HEADERS AND FOOTERS**

Very often it is useful to have not just a page number on a page but a piece of text alongside it to indicate perhaps a chapter heading or other information. A telephone directory, for example, has a header on each page telling the reader the first and last names on that page. Most word processors allow you to specify these things. Figure 3.7 shows a page with a header only, Figure 3.8 a page with a footer only and Figure 3.9 a page with both. Notice that they can incorporate the page number if required.

3.6 **PITCHES AND TYPEFACES**

A good example of the flexibility of a modern word processor coupled to a dot matrix printer is the ease with which you can *change the look of the text*. This can be done in a combination of ways. You can change the pitch of the characters, or you can change the typeface or font.

Pitch is the number of characters printed per inch, 10 pitch being 10 characters per inch, 12 pitch being 12 to the inch and 15 pitch being 15 to the inch. It is obvious, therefore, that the higher the pitch number the more *condensed* the characters are. Figure 3.10 shows text in these three pitches. They are the commonest pitches in use. If a daisy wheel printer is used pitch change is achieved by replacing one daisy wheel with another. If you have a dot matrix printer then the pitch change is embedded as a command in the text and is totally under the control of the software.

Fig 3.5 *An "orphan"*

1

In a letter to a woman's magazine recently a reader wrote that she was frightened of computers and that

> I was told by a computer addict that my plans for becoming an interpreter were pointless. He said that wordprocessors would soon replace the human....

First of all I should like to reassure the lady that her fears are quite groundless. One can gauge the quality of the advice given by the adviser being described as a 'computer addict'. These so-called experts are among the worst advocates of the new technology and are prone to cloud the real issues with mythology and mumbo-jumbo. No wonder the average adult person is terrified of anything to do with computers. Of course, the popular press and television do not help a lot either. The advice the reader has been given was unfortunately typical of wrong thinking by the so-called computer enthusiasts who have a very narrow and highly coloured view of what computers can and cannot do. It is certainly unlikely in our lifetime, or even our children's, that computers will replace humans; at least in the sense that the writer

2

of that rather pathetic letter fears.
　　There is no doubt that computers are already performing tasks which humans traditionally have done for many years. For example, quite small and cheap computers can handle all the invoicing and keep track of the financial transactions of a business; surely that can be no bad thing.
　　Computers can help in financial planning - cash flow projections for example

Fig 3.6 *Protecting "widows" and "orphans"*

1

In a letter to a woman's magazine recently a
reader wrote that she was frightened of
computers and that

> I was told by a computer addict that my
> plans for becoming an interpreter were
> pointless. He said that wordprocessors
> would soon replace the human....

First of all I should like to reassure the
lady that her fears are quite groundless. One
can gauge the quality of the advice given by
the adviser being described as a 'computer
addict'. These so-called experts are among
the worst advocates of the new technology and
are prone to cloud the real issues with
mythology and mumbo-jumbo. No wonder the
average adult person is terrified of anything
to do with computers. Of course, the popular
press and television do not help a lot either.
The advice the reader has been given was
unfortunately typical of wrong thinking by the
so-called computer enthusiasts who have a very
narrow and highly coloured view of what
computers can and cannot do. It is certainly
unlikely in our lifetime, or even our
children's' that computers will replace

2

humans; at least in the sense that the writer
of that rather pathetic letter fears.
There is no doubt that computers are
already performing tasks which humans
traditionally have done for many years. For
example, quite small and cheap computers can
handle all the invoicing and keep track of the
financial transactions of a business; surely
that can be no bad thing.
Computers can help in financial planning
- cash flow projections for example

Fig 3.7 *A header*

In a letter to a woman's magazine recently a
reader wrote that she was frightened of
computers and that

I was told by a computer addict that my
plans for becoming an interpreter were
pointless. He said that wordprocessors
would soon replace the human....

First of all I should like to reassure the
lady that her fears are quite groundless. One
can gauge the quality of the advice given by
the adviser being described as a 'computer
addict'. These so-called experts are among
the worst advocates of the new technology and
are prone to cloud the real issues with
mythology and mumbo-jumbo. No wonder the
average adult person is terrified of anything
to do with computers. Of course, the popular
press and television do not help a lot either.
The advice the reader has been given was
unfortunately typical of wrong thinking by the
so-called computer enthusiasts who have a very
narrow and highly coloured view of what
computers can and cannot do. It is certainly
unlikely in our lifetime, or even our
children's, that computers will replace

humans; at least in the sense that the writer
of that rather pathetic letter fears.
 There is no doubt that computers are
already performing tasks which humans
traditionally have done for many years. For
example, quite small and cheap computers can
handle all the invoicing and keep track of the
financial transactions of a business; surely
that can be no bad thing.
 Computers can help in financial planning
- cash flow projections for example

46

Fig 3.8 *A footer*

In a letter to a woman's magazine recently a
reader wrote that she was frightened of
computers and that

I was told by a computer addict that my
plans for becoming an interpreter were
pointless. He said that wordprocessors
would soon replace the human....

First of all I should like to reassure the
lady that her fears are quite groundless. One
can gauge the quality of the advice given by
the adviser being described as a 'computer
addict'. These so-called experts are among
the worst advocates of the new technology and
are prone to cloud the real issues with
mythology and mumbo-jumbo. No wonder the
average adult person is terrified of anything
to do with computers. Of course, the popular
press and television do not help a lot either.
The advice the reader has been given was
unfortunately typical of wrong thinking by the
so-called computer enthusiasts who have a very
narrow and highly coloured view of what
computers can and cannot do. It is certainly
unlikely in our lifetime, or even our
children's, that computers will replace

humans; at least in the sense that the writer
of that rather pathetic letter fears.
    There is no doubt that computers are
already performing tasks which humans
traditionally have done for many years. For
example, quite small and cheap computers can
handle all the invoicing and keep track of the
financial transactions of a business; surely
that can be no bad thing.
    Computers can help in financial planning
- cash flow projections for example

Fig 3.9 *A header and a footer*

Chapter 1   1

   In a letter to a woman's magazine recently a
   reader wrote that she   was frightened of
   computers and that

      I was told by a computer addict that my
      plans for becoming an interpreter were
      pointless.   He said that wordprocessors
      would soon replace the human....

   First of all I should like to reassure the
   lady that her fears are quite groundless. One
   can gauge the quality of the advice given by
   the adviser being described as a 'computer
   addict'. These so-called experts are among
   the worst advocates of the new technology and
   are prone to cloud the real issues with
   mythology and mumbo-jumbo.   No wonder the
   average adult person is terrified of anything
   to do with computers. Of course, the popular
   press and television do not help a lot either.
   The advice the reader has been given was
   unfortunately typical of wrong thinking by the
   so-called computer enthusiasts who have a very
   narrow and highly coloured view of what
   computers can and cannot do. It is certainly
   unlikely in our lifetime, or even our

Mastering Wordprocessing

Chapter 1   2

   children's, that computers will replace
   humans; at least in the sense that the writer
   of that rather pathetic letter fears.
      There is no doubt that computers are
   already performing tasks which humans
   traditionally have done for many years. For
   example, quite small and cheap computers can
   handle all the invoicing and keep track of the
   financial transactions of a business; surely
   that can be no bad thing.
      Computers can help in financial planning
   - cash flow projections for example

Fig 3.10 *Pitch of characters*

This is in 10 pitch

This is in 12 pitch

This is in 15 pitch

Fig 3.11 *Typefaces*

Dot matrix printers offer a wide range

Dot matrix printers offer a wide range

Dot matrix printers offer a wide range

Dot matrix printers offer a wide range

matrix printers offe

matrix printers off

Dot matrix printers offer a wide range

Dot matrix printers offer a wide range

There are thousands of different fonts or typefaces used in the printing trade known by names such as Times Roman, Italic Bold, Script and many others. Because a dot matrix printer forms its characters by the pattern of dots it fires onto the paper it can make a very good attempt at copying some of these. Obviously the larger the number of dots the greater the variety of fonts available. If you are using a daisy wheel printer, as with a pitch change, you would have to stop the printing in order to change the wheel whenever you wished to change the font. The advantage that this has over the dot matrix system is that by having a large number of daisy wheels you have access to a very wide range of typefaces. The disadvantage is that daisy wheels are quite expensive. Figure 3.11 shows a selection of typefaces available. The example shown in Figure 3.12 shows the effect that can be produced by including a change of both pitch and typeface within a piece of text. A second piece of text shown in Figure 3.13. The first paragraph in that figure is the standard default pitch and font, but justified.

You will find that when you are using proportional spacing you may see some strange side effects. These are most commonly seen in the way that the program's adherence to tab stops can go awry in a spectacular manner under these conditions. If you change the pitch of a portion of your text you can find that this, too, can have strange effects on the layout of your page. Change pitch or typeface and you can find that centred text becomes centred no longer just as tab stops lose their meaning. These anomalies are not common to all word processors, but if you have the need for proportional spacing and constant pitch changes then make sure that the word processor you buy will take these changes in its stride.

One of the problems associated with the presentation of text produced by a word processor is that different letters have different widths, but this is not always taken account of the printer. This was mentioned briefly in Section 3.1. If the technique of proportional spacing is used the look of the finished text is much enhanced since account is taken of the different sizes of the characters and the spaces between words; these are all

Fig 3.12 *Changing pitch and typeface*

In a letter to a woman's magazine recently a
reader wrote that she was frightened of
computers and that

> I was told by a computer addict that my plans for
> becoming an interpreter were pointless. He said
> that wordprocessors would soon replace the
> human....

First of all I should like to reassure the
lady that her fears are quite groundless. One
can gauge the quality of the advice given by
the adviser being described as a 'computer
addict'. These so-called experts are among
the worst advocates of the new technology and
are prone to cloud the real issues with
mythology and mumbo-jumbo. No wonder the
average adult person is terrified of anything
to do with computers. Of course, the popular
press and television do not help a lot either.
The advice the reader has been given was
unfortunately typical of wrong thinking by the
so-called computer enthusiasts who have a very
narrow and highly coloured view of what
computers can and cannot do. It is certainly
unlikely in our lifetime, or even our
children's, that computers will replace
humans; at least in the sense that the writer

evened out if proportional spacing is used. A number of
word processors allow you to do this, and the result of
using proportional spacing together with justification
is shown in the second piece of text in Figure 3.13.

Fig 3.13 *Changing pitch and typeface, and the effect of justification and proportional spacing*

One of the reasons for using computers is that they can relieve us of dull, boring and repetitive jobs and give them to a machine which is quite happy performing this type of task.   This provides us with the freedom to think about the things which really matter and offers us a way of improving the quality of life.

One of the reasons for using computers is that they can relieve us of dull, boring and repetitive jobs and give them to a machine which is quite happy performing this type of task. This provides us with the freedom to think about the things which really matter and offers us a way of improving the quality of life.

3.7 **SUBSCRIPTS, SUPERSCRIPTS AND SPECIAL EFFECTS**

If you have a need to do any scientific work on your word processor then you may well have to be able to produce *mathematical or scientific formulas*. In these you very often require the print characters not on the current line of printing, but slightly above or below that line.

For example, a temperature such as $30^{\circ}C$ can be produced by superscripting a lower case letter "o". And a chemical formula such as H_2SO_4 uses subscripted figures 2 and 4. Some of the simpler word processors produce subscripts and superscripts by printing the characters on a blank line below or above the current line. More sophisticated word processors, as in Figure 3.14, actually print smaller characters in the appropriate place.

Various other effects can be produced by a similar effect where **overprinting** of characters takes place. This means that instead of the printing head moving onto the next space before printing it remains in the same place and prints one character over the one it has just printed. Thus it is possible to produce arrows by over printing the > character with a dash - and then printing several more after it to achieve the effect. ---> . A number of examples using subscripts, superscripts and overstriking are shown in Figure 3.14.

Fig 3.14 *Arrows, subscripts, superscripts and overstriking*

$$X^3 + 3X^2 + X - 2 = 0$$

$$\frac{sec^2 2X}{2}$$

$$CH_3COOH$$

$$W_{max} = I_{max} \ X \ V_{max}$$

$$\begin{array}{c} \uparrow \\ \longleftarrow ---- \ --- \longrightarrow \\ \downarrow \end{array}$$

Special effects, such as producing French accents or characters that do not normally appear on an English keyboard can be created by using overprinting techniques. The French circumflex can be placed over a word by overprinting the ^ character in order to produce the word **côte**.

3.8 LINES AND BOXES

With the right dot matrix printer you can draw lines and boxes in your text so that you can produce *tables and charts*. These lines and boxes can then be reproduced by the printer which goes into a special mode called "graphics mode" as it draws the lines. The examples shown in Figures 3.15 and 3.16 illustrate line drawing used in the in-house documentation for a company. The second of the examples shows a blank form produced ready for completion.

Figure 3.17 shows an organisational chart drawn using the word processor and printed by a dot matrix printer. In Figure 3.17 the boxes have been drawn first and then the text has been inserted afterwards using overtype mode. This is the best way to approach the creation of this type of word processor output. If you do it like that you have less chance of the output being corrupted by an excess of carriage returns. Remember that when you are using overtype mode you should move the cursor across the screen by means of the *space bar*, a space is

Fig 3.15 *Company documentation*

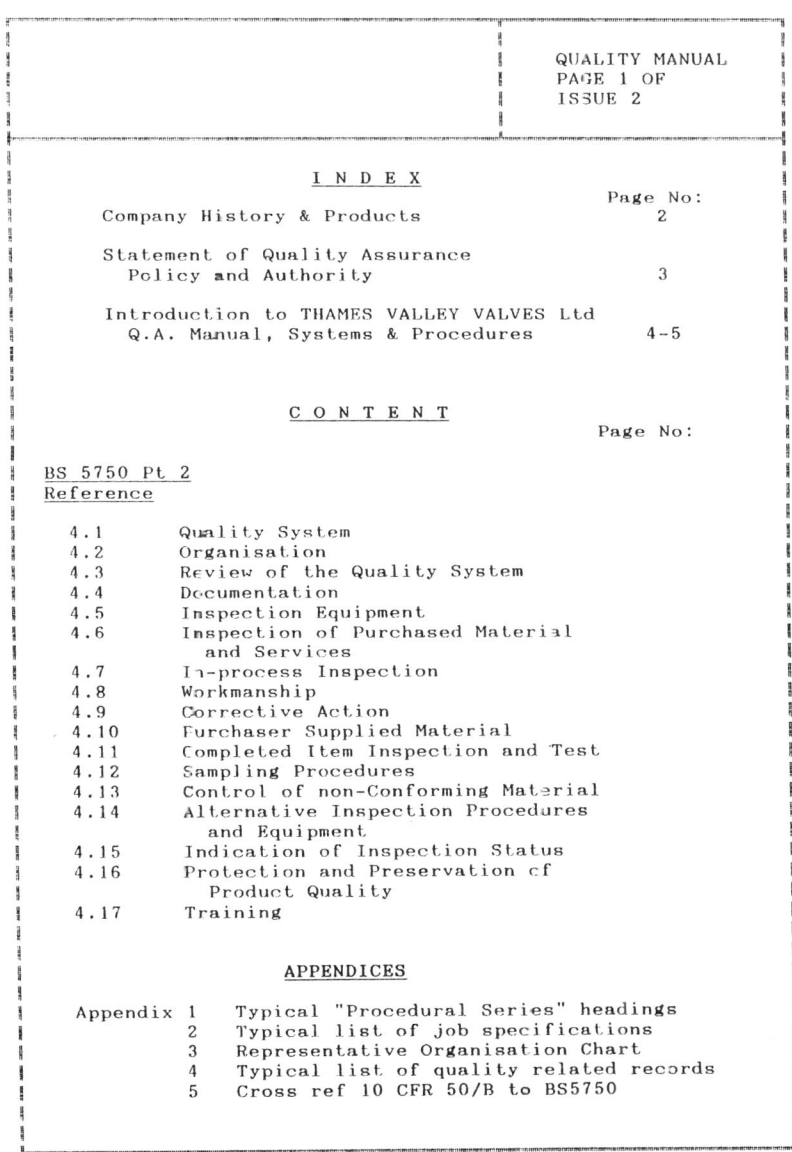

```
                                          QUALITY MANUAL
                                          PAGE 1 OF
                                          ISSUE 2


                        I N D E X
                                               Page No:
           Company History & Products              2

           Statement of Quality Assurance
              Policy and Authority                 3

           Introduction to THAMES VALLEY VALVES Ltd
              Q.A. Manual, Systems & Procedures    4-5



                        C O N T E N T
                                               Page No:

        BS 5750 Pt 2
        Reference

           4.1       Quality System
           4.2       Organisation
           4.3       Review of the Quality System
           4.4       Documentation
           4.5       Inspection Equipment
           4.6       Inspection of Purchased Material
                        and Services
           4.7       In-process Inspection
           4.8       Workmanship
           4.9       Corrective Action
           4.10      Purchaser Supplied Material
           4.11      Completed Item Inspection and Test
           4.12      Sampling Procedures
           4.13      Control of non-Conforming Material
           4.14      Alternative Inspection Procedures
                        and Equipment
           4.15      Indication of Inspection Status
           4.16      Protection and Preservation of
                        Product Quality
           4.17      Training


                        APPENDICES

        Appendix 1    Typical "Procedural Series" headings
                 2    Typical list of job specifications
                 3    Representative Organisation Chart
                 4    Typical list of quality related records
                 5    Cross ref 10 CFR 50/B to BS5750
```

Fig 3.16 *Blank form for company documentation*

JOB SPECIFICATION	REF No JS/ ISSUE DATE 22/9/88 REVISION 2

Job Title:

Present Holder:

Responsible to:

Responsible for:

----

a character and will erase characters as you move. You can use the *arrow keys* to move you about if you do not wish to erase by using the space bar. Do not use the **RETURN** key while you are in overtype mode.

Fig 3.17 *Organisational chart : **overtype** mode in pre-drawn boxes*

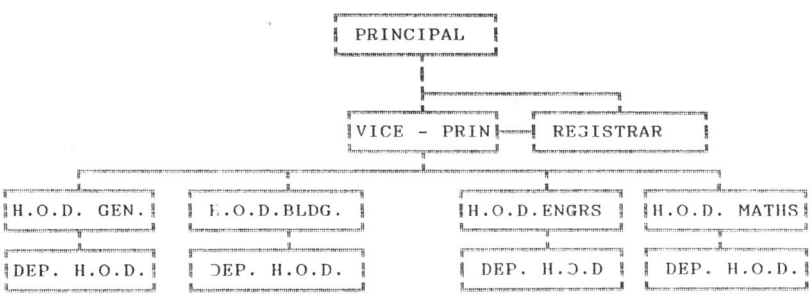

3.9 **FOOTNOTES AND ENDNOTES**

In many technical papers and books it is necessary to annotate the text by means of footnotes. To do it manually requires a knowledge of the layout of the page and the relationship between the line of text containing the reference and the footnote itself. A good word processor will allow you to mark the text for a footnote and will automatically allocate space at the bottom of the page for the footnote text. The example shown in Figure 3.18 shows a page from a document giving five footnotes at the bottom of the page. The footnotes will be automatically numbered for you throughout the document, so that the effort required on your part is quite small.

If you wish the footnotes for one document, or chapter of a book, could be collected together as *endnotes* by the word processor, so that instead of being printed at the bottom of each page they are placed at the end of the text.

Fig 3.18 *Document and footnotes*

NATURAL HISTORY

The epidemic of pulmonary hypertension due to the appetite suppressant aminorex is now over[1]. Only one person in 1000 exposed to this drug developed pulmonary hypertension suggesting individual predisposition. The association between the dose and response in affected subjects was found to be poor[2]. Ten-year survival was better than for patients with primary hypertension, 60% having haemodynamic and clinical improvement. Survival is clearly related to absence of right heart failure and lower pulmonary vascular resistance, which is also shown for primary pulmonary hypertension[3] as well as for pulmonary embolism[4].

The finding of spontaneous regression of pulmonary hypertension and long-term reduction of pulmonary vascular resistance in hypoxic lung disease following oxygen therapy or vascodilators treatment[5], gives encouragement to clinicians. Whether pulmonary vascular resistance ever returns entirely to normal in these conditions, both at rest and on exercise, remains to be seen. Even in pulmonary embolism where resolution of arterial obstruction by clot fibrinolysis is usually complete, there is evidence of permanent loss of gas exchange capacity. Lung function in patients without apparent pulmonary hypertension has been related to life expectancy. In a 24-year follow-up study of adult males, of those who had never smoked, the groups with lower predicted values of FEV_1 had greater mortality from all causes. It is suggested that the ability of the lung to

---

[1] Gurtner HP: Aminorex and pulmonary hypertension. A review. Cor Vasa 27:160–171.

[2] Loogen F, Worth H, Schwan G: Long-term follow-up primary vascular pulmonary hypertension in patients with and without anorectic drug intake. Cor Vas 1985, 27:111–124.

[3] Rozkovec A, Montanes P: Factors that influence the'outcome of primary pulmonart hypertension. Br Heart J 1986, 55:449–458.

[4] Benotti JR, Dalen JE: The natural history of pulmonary embolism. Clin Chest Med 1984, 5:403–410.

[5] Kennedy TP, Michael JR, Summer W: Calcium channel blockers in hypoxic pulmonary hypertension. Am Med J, 78(suppl 2B):18–26.

3.10 **ARITHMETIC**

Many word processors offer some form of arithmetic
functions in addition to their manipulation of characters. It will usually be of a fairly simple kind, but
you do have the opportunity to have the facilities of an
elementary spreadsheet. The usual kind of functions
offered will be to provide the totals of columns or rows
of figures and sub-totals as well. In Figure 3.19 you
will see a simple shopping list which consists of the
names of the items bought, their individual cost and the
number purchased. Then on the right is the cost of that
commodity - found by multiplying the item cost by the
number bought. The word processor is told the operation
to carry out, "multiply the contents of the second
column by the contents of the third". At the bottom of
this column is the total.

Fig 3.19 *A shopping list*

```
                    Shopping List

        Tea              .88      3        2.64
        Coffee          1.89      1        1.89
        Sugar            .45      3        1.35
        Butter           .65      1        0.65
        Milk             .26      3        0.78
        Bread            .55      2        1.10
        Flour            .87      1        0.87
        Cheese          1.56      2        3.12
        Bacon            .88      1        0.88
        Cereal           .79      2        1.58
        Washing Powder  1.60      1        1.60
                                         ------
                         Total:          16.46
                                         ------
```

Fig 3.20 *A shopping list recalculated*

```
                    Shopping List

        Tea              .88      3        2.64
        Coffee          1.89      1        1.89
        Sugar            .45      3        1.35
        Butter           .65      2        1.30
        Milk             .26      3        0.78
        Bread            .55      2        1.10
        Flour            .87      1        0.87
        Cheese          1.56      1        1.56
        Bacon            .88      1        0.88
        Cereal           .79      2        1.58
        Washing Powder  1.60      1        1.60
                                         ------
                         Total:          15.55
                                         ------
```

You will find that it is a very simple operation to tell the word processor to carry out the calculations and it is also easy to change any of the figures and do a recalculation with the result shown in Figure 3.20.

Although you have nothing like the functions available on a full-blown spreadsheet program you are able to produce simple bills and invoices and statements of account using the mathematical facilities offered by a number of the latest word processors. If you want to use more powerful facilities then you can always use a system (of a sort to be described later in this book) which has as part of the same program, word processing, spreadsheet, data handling and graphics facilities. All these can produce separate documents that can be collected together in one common document for the printing of a comprehensive *company report*.

3.11 HYPHENATION, LINE ADJUST AND THE "HOT ZONE"

When you use a typewriter, you use your own intuition to decide whether to *split a word* across two lines or not. Your decision affects the look of the page so that you can obtain a more or less justified right-hand edge without going to the trouble of counting spaces in order to produce a perfect right-hand margin.

Word processors have a "hot zone" of six to eight characters at the right-hand end of every line. When a word enters this zone it will be kept on the line if the end of the word falls within it. If, on the other hand, it exceeds the number of characters allotted to it in the hot zone then word wrap will take place unless you wish to hyphenate the word. Some word processors let you set the size of the hot zone. As a result of this a ragged right margin can look really ragged and justified text can be produced with just two words on a line, one at either end. Sometimes hyphenation is the answer.

The simplest form of hyphenation is to use a "soft hyphen" at the place in a word where a hyphen could occur if necessary. However, if a word that contains a

soft hyphen comes in the middle of a line the hyphen
will be hidden.

Some word processors contain a *hyphenation program.*
This is a set of instructions that tell the computer
under what circumstances a word may be hyphenated and
where the hyphen can come. This program will use a
dictionary that contains words that may be hyphenated,
and how. If the word is not found in the dictionary the
word will not be hyphenated.

Your word processor can be instructed, usually, to
hyphenate automatically or to give you the option of
hyphenating possible words or not. The example shown in
Figure 3.21 shows the effect of this. In the first
paragraph automatic hyphenation has been switched on and
you can see the effect on several of the lines. In the
second paragraph hyphenation has been switched off and
the increased "ragged" effect can be seen.

Fig 3.21 *Text with and without automatic hyphenation*

```
Much of the power of computers is going to be placed
at the disposal of people who work in offices.  By
the use of facilities such as word processing it is
possible to eliminate much of the boring repetitious
copy typing which is now done.  In addition there is
going to be the facility of having a cluster of com-
puters connected together in what is called a 'local
area network'.  This means that the computers all
have common access to files of data.  It is only a
short step to having computers connected together over
telephone lines.  This means that many executives
need visit their offices only infrequently as they
will have direct connection to all the data and pri-
nting facilities they require from their home where
they will have a computer terminal from which they
will be able to conduct the majority of their business.
```

```
Much of the power of computers is going to be placed
at the disposal of people who work in offices.  By
the use of facilities such as word processing it is
possible to eliminate much of the boring repetitious
copy typing which is now done.  In addition there is
going to be the facility of having a cluster of
computers connected together in what is called a
'local area network'.  This means that the computers
all have common access to files of data.  It is only
a short step to having computers connected together
over telephone lines.  This means that many executives
only need visit their offices infrequently as they
will have direct connection to all the data and
printing facilities they require from their home
where they will have a computer terminal from which
they will be able to conduct the majority of their
business.
```

3.12 **MACROS**

A macro is a *shortcut way* of doing some operation involving a number of keystrokes by reducing their number to a minimum. A good example of a macro in everyday use is on one of the latest pushbutton telephones. Many of these have a memory that can store many of your most used numbers. Pressing a recall button plus an identifying number will cause the call to be dialled automatically. You have just used a "macro" operation to do that!

In many word processors you have the facility to define a macro, such as a constantly used address or a regularly used command, and then record it under a simple one- or two- letter name. Then you can recall the complete piece of text or complicated command whenever you wish. It has the advantage not only of saving time but also of eliminating the possibility of error when typing in a lengthy entry. You can often use macros for the closing paragraphs of letters, for example

Yours sincerely

John Beecham

Product Manager

or for the date, which will either be changed automatically by the computer system each day, or changed by you at the start of every day. This depends on the word processor you are using. Some of them will automatically keep track of what is called the "system date". Another use of macros would be to store regularly-used technical terms or lengthy medical names. Such things as, for example

pulmonary hypertension

cross-sectional echocardiography

or even

antidisestablishmentarianism

3.13 KEYBOARD EXTENSIONS

Most word processors will configure for either American or English keyboards. As a result the pound sign may often appear as a dollar, but more often as a hash symbol (#). But what can you do if you need to write a letter to a French person, or include Greek letters in a formula? A *keyboard extension* is used to access characters that do not appear on a standard "qwerty" keyboard. Sometimes you will need to reassign the **Control** or **Alt** keys so that an â is produced when **Alt a** is pressed, for example. Sometimes you will need to use a control code followed by the *hexadecimal code* to generate the character. Other systems access special characters in other ways but it is usually possible. The simplest way to produce an *accent* over a character is to use the *overprint command*. So, if you wanted to produce â you would key-in **a**, use the overprint command and key-in ^.

3.14 WINDOWS

If you wanted to look at two documents at the same time then you would have to "open a window". This *splits the workscreen*, usually in half; the original document will be displayed in one window and the other will be blank. You can now move the cursor into the empty window and retrieve another file in the usual way. A window becomes "current" when the cursor is in it. You can use each document in the normal way. There is no difference between a document in a window and a document that fills the entire workscreen.

This feature is invaluable when you want to copy chunks of text from one document to another. It is also useful if you want to refer to one document while working on another. Perhaps you had created a contents list and needed to follow it. You can now display it in a window and keep it there while you work; see the example in

Figure 3.22. You can even put parts of the same document into windows.

 When you want to "close a window" you will usually need to put the cursor in that window and issue the **save** command. The window will now "close" and the remaining document will fill the workscreen.

Fig 3.22 *Text displayed in a window*

1   Introduction

2   Contents

3   Create and Print a Simple Letter

4   Tabs and Margins
                                                    Doc 1
L----!------------------------------------R
1   Introduction

This handbook has been designed to fill a very
real gap in the market. The manufacturers'
manuals tend to be lengthy and confusing.
Moreover, most of the topics covered will be
of no use to you. Here at Macmillan Education
we have recognised this and have devised the
Macmillan Modern Office Series. Now you can
introduce yourself to a program in easy steps.
You can teach yourself with MMO and proceed as
quickly, or as slowly, as you like. The
manuals are inexpensive and in exercise book
                                                    Doc 2

3.15 **SPELLER**

Not only does a word processor stop you having to retype a whole page when one tiny mistake is discovered but it can also check your spelling! (Nevertheless don't expect it to notice the times when you typed "here" instead of "hear" by accident!)

 There are two main types of spelling check. Earlier programs tended to compare each word that was not recognised by its dictionary and then "flag" that word. A flag could be a special symbol at the start of each unrecognised word or the word could be highlighted. It was then up to the operator to recheck the flagged words. Some word processors still operate in this way, (this is the case for MultiMate Advantage). In which case a spell edit should be carried out. A spell edit will find each flagged word and make suggestions as to the correct spelling. You then select the *correct suggestion* from the list. If there is no appropriate alternative you can key-in the correction yourself.

Many word processor miss out the flagging process altogether and offer alternative spellings straight away.

Spell check programs use one or more *dictionaries*. Often there will be one (shorter) dictionary that will contain a common word list, the idea being that the computer will look in this list first and help speed things up a bit. There will then be a second (larger) dictionary, often about 100,000 words long, which will be used to find words that were not in the common word list. A third kind of dictionary is called a "personal dictionary". This is *created by you* and will contain all the words that you know to be correct but that the dictionary cannot recognise, such as the name of your company, surnames or place names. Words can be added to a personal dictionary during the spelling check. Often you can revise a personal dictionary like a normal document and add words directly to it. Most word processors allow you to create as many personal dict-ionaries as you like and "attach" the relevant one during the spell check.

Some word processors can offer *phonetic alternatives* to the unrecognized word. You would be amazed how often you key-in a word twice by accident and some programs pick this up too. It is wise to check a document yourself afterwards, just to pick up words that are correctly spelt but still incorrect - "their" instead of "there" for example.

Often you do not need to check the whole document. Many programs allow you to check the spelling of a single word, a sentence, a paragraph, a page, a marked block of text or even a chapter. Often a word count will be displayed after the text has been checked.

3.16 **THESAURUS**

Authors will find the Thesaurus program invaluable. You will usually be able to highlight the word you want to look up and then ask the Thesaurus to give you some alternatives. Synonyms and antonyms will be offered. In fact it is easier to use than **Roget** because you do not have to keep looking for the correct page. Instead you can pick a word from the list you are offered and look that one up straight away.

SUMMARY

1. *Justification* provides you with a straight right hand margin.
2. A *tab* moves the cursor to a pre-defined column. Text is indented when it starts at a column after the normal left hand edge of the text.
3. *Pagination* sets the text within the top and bottom margins of each page.
4. An *orphan* is a line of text on its own at the top of a page.
5. A *widow* is a line of text left all alone at the bottom of a page.
6. A *header* is a repeated pice of text, often containing a page number, printed at the top of every page.
7. A *footer* is a repeated piece of text, often containing a page number, printed at the bottom of every page.
8. Text can be printed in different *typefaces* (letter shapes) and different *fonts* (character width).
9. A *subscript* is a character printed below the current line of text.
10. A *superscript* is a character printed above the current line of text.
11. A *footnote* is printed at the bottom of a page with a reference to an entry on that page.
12. An *endnote* is printed at the end of a document referring to an entry in that document.

13. *Hyphenation* can either be decided by you or left to the word processor program.
14. A *macro* reduces the entry of an often repeated set of key strokes to the depression of one or two keys only.
15. A *window* allows you to edit two documents at the same time.
16. A *spell check* will compare the words in your document with one or more dictionaries and help you to correct unmatched words.
17. A *Thesaurus* will offer synonyms and antonyms.

MAILING LISTS

Word processors make an easy task of producing, maintaining and distributing sets of letters that differ only in details such as the name, address and possibly some variable format. This type of letter drops through the letter box regularly these days, offering free entry to competitions, book club subscriptions and many other things packaged in such a way as to make the letter appear personal and targeted at you and you alone. The techniques used to create these letters are very simple. The hard part, and that is not so very hard anyway, is *getting the lists of people* to whom these offers are aimed. In the commercial world mailing lists are not difficult to come by at the right price - it is not difficult in fact to purchase a list of all those people in a certain social group who have bought, for example, a lawnmower in the past six months. Armed with such a list you stand a very good chance of selling lawn care products to these people. This is a far more efficient way of advertising your wares than by picking names at random out of the telephone directory. In America, for example, there are catalogues of mailing lists that offer lists of people in every conceivable walk of life, age group, social group, income group and location. You can then purchase the list you want already on a disk or tape ready for merging with your letter.

4.1   MERGE LETTERS AND DATA FILES

The two things you need in order to send out your "mail shot" are a list of names and addresses and a letter drafted to send to each of these people. The list of names and addresses constitute a "data file" and the word processor program will then *integrate* each separate name and address into a letter that has been prepared with gaps in it ready to receive the names and addresses. This is the "merge letter". The two documents-the data file and the merge letter - are then automatically brought together and printed. Each letter ends up being printed with a unique name and address ready for distribution through the post to the target customer.

One of the simplest mailing list functions is the one offered by the WordStar word processor. The data file, as they all do, simply consists of a list of names and addresses arranged in *sets*. The *structure* of these sets is always of great importance. Each set, or "record", must consist of exactly the correct number of "fields"; these fields can be made up in any way you wish, but for the example given here they consist of nine pieces of information. The first field contains the *surname*, the second the *title* (Mr, Mrs, Ms, etc.), the third consists of the *initials*. The next four fields are the four lines of the *address* and the last two are the *postcode* and the *telephone number*. If, for example, there are only three address lines for one particular entry then one of the address fields must be left blank: computer programs get very confused if you do not lay out information in a totally unambiguous way. A section from such a data file is shown in Figure 4.1. You should notice that the first entry has only three address fields and so there is a blank field after the county (Berks) signified by the comma that ends the field being followed by another comma immediately. This shows that the field is there, but empty. The same thing happens in the third entry as well.

The blank letter that is going to be filled with the data is shown in Figure 4.2. It commences with three lines that are of great importance. The first of these that starts off with the code

.DF

Fig 4.1 *Mailing list data file*

```
Agnew,Mr,AJ,14 Meadowbank Road,READING,Berks,,RG20 4XT,0256 34213
Blake,Mrs,L,"The Limes",Crown Lane,CAMBRIDGE,Cambs,CB3 3RT,0223 21245
Cooper,Miss,A,12 Wilson Crescent,HUNTINGDON,Cambs,,PE19 1DF,0480 6754
```

Fig 4.2 *Blank mailing list letter*

```
.DF MAIL1.DAT
.RV NAME,TITLE,INITS,ADDR1,ADDR2,ADDR3,ADDR4,PC,PHONE
.OP
```

```
1 January 1988


&TITLE& &INITS& &NAME&
&ADDR1&
&ADDR2&
&ADDR3&
&ADDR4& &PC&

Dear &TITLE& &NAME&

I should like to inform you of our fabulous new offer
which is available to you, &TITLE& &NAME&, only. Won't
your friends in &ADDR2& be envious of you when you drive
up in your new 1988 THUNDERER sports car!  All you have
to do is answer the six simple questions on the attached
form and the chance, &TITLE& &NAME&, is yours.


Best wishes and good luck

SPARKELWITE TOOTHPASTE COMPANY
```

which specifies the *data file* to be used in conjunction with the letter that follows. The name of the file - and there could be several to choose from in the word processing system - is **MAIL1.DAT**. The second line specifies the *name* by which each field is to be known so that each field can be placed in the correct place in the letter. This is done by a line that starts with

.RV

The third command

.OP

is to tell WordStar not to print a page number at the end of the letter.

You should notice that the telephone number is not actually used in the letter. Even though it is not used in this case the word processor *must know that it is there* - computers are pretty stupid after all! The fields are defined by the name of the field enclosed within a pair of **&** symbols so that **&TITLE& &NAME&** will enter, for example,

Mr Agnew

into the letter, whereas **&TITLE& &INITS& &NAME&** will enter

Mr AJ Agnew

The fields can be entered wherever you wish in the letter, in any order and repeated as many times as you wish as you can see in Figure 4.2. The final results, shown for the three lines of data illustrated, are shown in Figure 4.3. There we have three individual letters - not copies - ready to be mailed. They can be mailed either in window envelopes or in envelopes with pre-printed labels stuck on them. The labels, of course, are produced in the same way as the letters, as is shown in Section 4.2.

Fig 4.3 *Completed mailing list letters*

```
1 January 1988

Miss A Cooper
12 Wilson Crescent
HUNTINGDON
Cambs
PE19 1DF

Dear Miss Cooper

I should like to inform you of our fabulous new offer
which is available to you, Miss Cooper, only. Won't
your friends in HUNTINGDON be envious of you when you
drive up in your new 1988 THUNDERER sports car!  All you
have to do is answer the six simple questions on the
attached form and the chance, Miss Cooper, is yours.


Best wishes and good luck

SPARKELWITE TOOTHPASTE COMPANY
```

Fig 4.3 *Continued*

1 January 1988

Mr AJ Agnew
14 Meadowbank Road
READING
Berks
RG20 4XT

Dear Mr Agnew

I should like to inform you of our fabulous new offer
which is available to you, Mr Agnew, only. Won't your
friends in READING be envious of you when you drive up
in your new 1988 THUNDERER sports car! All you have to
do is answer the six simple questions on the attached
form and the chance, Mr Agnew, is yours.

Best wishes and good luck

SPARKELWITE TOOTHPASTE COMPANY

----

1 January 1988

Mrs L Blake
The Limes
Crown Lane
CAMBRIDGE
Cambs CB2 3RT

Dear Mrs Blake

I should like to inform you of our fabulous new offer
which is available to you, Mrs Blake, only. Won't your
friends in CAMBRIDGE be envious of you when you drive up
in your new 1988 THUNDERER sports car! All you have to
do is answer the six simple questions on the attached
form and the chance, Mrs Blake, is yours.

Best wishes and good luck

SPARKELWITE TOOTHPASTE COMPANY

4.2 LABEL PRINTING

The preparation of addressed envelopes to go with a mailing list operation presents a number of problems to be overcome. The first of these is that printing addresses on *single envelopes* one at a time is out of the question. Apart from the fact that envelopes are not easy to feed into most printers and when they are in (because of their thickness) they do not scroll up properly to receive each line of the address, feeding envelopes one at a time is very wasteful. Envelopes in continuous strips like fan-fold paper are available but are bound to be more expensive than conventional envelopes. The real answer is to use *peelable labels* that can be purchased in strips as with fan-fold paper. They come in several forms. One is on a narrow strip of waxed paper one label wide; this is the simplest to print onto as most word processors with a mail-merge facility can be made to print onto this type of label. A set of instructions, in WordStar again, for label printing is shown in Figure 4.4. The first three lines are

Fig 4.4 *WordStar instructions for label printing*

```
.DF MAIL1.DAT
.RV NAME,TITLE,INITS,ADDR1,ADDR2,ADDR3,ADDR4,PC,PHONE
.OP
.PL
.PO10
.MT0
.MB8

&TITLE& &INITS& &NAME
&ADDR1&
&ADDR2&
&ADDR3&
&ADDR4&
&PC&
.PA
```

exactly the same as in the merge letter but they are followed by instructions that tell WordStar that they are dealing with *very short pages*, the label in fact. Each label is only nine lines deep (the A4 page usually used is 66 lines deep). The command

.PL9

defines the Length of the "Page". The command

.PO10

is a "Page Offset" command that tells WordStar to start printing not at the extreme left-hand edge of the label but *ten characters* in. The next two commands

.MT0

and

.MB0

tell WordStar that there are no top or bottom margins to be left. This is because most word processors will normally leave quite large margins at the top and bottom of a document, this is in order to take account of possible headers, footers or page numbers. Labels do not require such things, so they are eliminated.

Labels are also available in sets of two, three or four across the page. This type of label is not so easy to print on some word processors, WordStar cannot handle them for example. Others can; WordStar[1512] (no relation except in name to WordStar), has the facility of coping with such an arrangement so that labels get printed faster when they are arranged as shown in Figure 4.5, known as "three-up" label printing.

Fig 4.5 *"Three-up" label printing*

Mr AJ Hibbins	Mrs J Smith	Ms K Goddard
12 The High Street	6 Lawn Avenue	Flat 2
Hightown	Grimwade Gardens	Asley Court
Cambs	Growthorpe	Tinsley
CB3 6BZ	HA6 8YQ	WA5 8YG
Mrs H Grice	Mr PT Grace	Mrs C Groce
High Trees	14 Willow Road	The Cosy Shop
Green Lane	Grisley	The Parade
Harply	Warwicks	Grenham
TA8 8BG	B19 7HG	PO7 9BC

One word of warning when using label printing. Be very careful that one of the labels does not *detach itself* from the waxed backing sheet and wind itself around the printer roller. This causes a number of problems. The first of these is that unsticking the errant label is not easy and secondly if you can detach it there is a residue of gum that is left behind on the roller. This immediately gives you problems when you come to print on ordinary paper. You will find that it will not feed through properly and will stick on the roller. The only solution, unfortunately, is to take the printer to a service engineer who will have to dismantle part of it to remove the roller which then has to be cleaned with spirit to get rid of the sticky mess.

4.3 SELECTING FROM A DATA FILE

Very often you will find that you want to send letters to only a part of your mailing list. This means that there must be some way of separating those addresses you want to be *ignored* from those you need to be *included*. Some word processors provide you with a function that enables you to mark those you want to select for mailing. MultiMate Advantage (see Glossary) for example, allows you to create each record as a separate entity so that it looks like a form that you fill in. Each of these "forms" can be Selected or Deselected. It is only those Selected records that are incorporated in the mailing list. WordStar[1512] is similar but takes the procedure a step further in that it allows you to prepare what is called a "mask" then ensures that, for example, letters are sent only to those people on the list whose town is Reading, whose position is Company Secretary and who have been flagged as having been visited in the last three months. A number of word processors will allow you to sort the data file into an order based on the surname, town or county or any other field in the file.

There are other ways of approaching the problem if you have a word processor that does not allow selection from a data list. This involves you in using another program - called a database program (see Glossary)- that will examine your files and make selections from them or sort them into order. Such a program would be dBASE II or dBASE III. The communication between a word processor and a database program is dealt with in Chapter 5.

SUMMARY

1. In order to produce a series of identical letters to a list of people you need a *data file* containing the names and addresses of the people to whom letters are to be sent.

2. A *blank letter* containing the text of the letter with "holes" in it to contain the names and addresses extracted from the *data file*.

3. The data file and the blank letter are then *merged* together to produce a series of *personalised* letters each one apparently individually typed.

4. The same data file can be merged with another blank document in order to produce a series of *address labels* for the envelopes.

INTEGRATED

PACKAGES

5.1 **WORD PROCESSORS, DATABASES AND SPREADSHEETS**

There are now a number of "packages" that combine all the features of several different programs. This allows a user to incorporate data from, say, a spreadsheet very simply into a report generated by a word processor without a lot of changing of programs. As you will see in Section 5.1 this makes it a very simple task to produce a complex document containing a number of separate parts. Two of the most popular programs of this type are Symphony and Framework. An earlier type of integrated program was T/Maker which was described in Chapter 5 of the first edition of *Mastering Word Processing*.

Programs of this type tend to adopt the "desktop" approach to computing. This turns your screen into a make-believe desk with filing cabinets, wastepaper baskets and scribbling pads. Documents are filed away in, and retrieved from, a "drawer" in the "filing cabinet" and consigned to the "waste bin" when discarded. By a simple sequence of keystrokes you can call a diagram into your document, design complicated sets of related documents and manipulate data in all manner of ways.

As the accent is on word processors in this book, a brief description of what you can expect from such a system if you want to create and print a document is the next step. The program used to create this example was Framework II.

Figure 5.1 shows the screen just before you start to type in the text of a document. Along the top you have a series of *command options* that you can select by using the arrow keys. The "**Numbers**" option gives you a menu of choices if you are going to perform some arithmetic using, for example, a spreadsheet. The "**Words**" option has been selected in Figure 5.1 providing you with the menu from which you can select a number of options when you want to start word processing in order for you to define the layout of your text. From the menu you can select the text style, alignment and margin and paragraph settings. Whenever you want to start emboldening or underlining you have to go to this menu and select the appropriate command, by using the arrow keys to move through the menu, and the **RETURN** key to select your requirement. Then you enter your text. Select the menu again and change the command back to what it was before. Once the technique of using menus of this sort has been mastered it is very easy to use. Issuing commands by menu selection is a feature of several popular word processors, WordStar[1512] (see Glossary) being one.

If you wish to do a search and replace operation on your text you can choose the "**Locate**" option which displays the menu as shown in Figure 5.2. By selecting the **Replace** choice you can tell Framework the character(s) you want searching for and the character(s) to be the replacement and then the program will take over.

When you have created your document you can print it by selecting "**Print**" and then "**Format Options**" which will give you the menu shown in Figure 5.3. You can see how you can specify how the document is to be printed by selecting the **Print Appearance** and any **Headers** and **Footers.** This all means that control of output is very simple.

Fig. 5.1 *Command options on the screen*

```
Apps  Disk  Create  Edit  Locate  Frames  Words  Numbers  Graph  Print  10:37 am

                                                              <Library>

                        -- Normal
                     on Bold                                  <A:>
                        -- Underline                          <B:>
                        -- Italic

                        -- Align Left
                        -- Flush Right
                        -- Justify
                        -- Center

                        -- Left Margin        {0}
                        -- Right Margin      {65}
                        -- Paragraph Indent   {0}
                        -- Tab Size           {5}


                  ||              ||  Cabinet:  3/3
                                B:

            Boldface selected text - in any type of frame
```

78

Fig. 5.2 *Displaying the menu*

```
Apps  Disk  Create  Edit  Locate  Frames  Words  Numbers  Graph  Print  10:39 am

                                                          <Library>

                                                              <A:>
                                                              <B:>

        Ascending Sort
        Descending Sort

        Search              {}
        Replace             {}
     on Labels Included
     on Contents Included
     -- Formulas Included

     on Ignore Capitalization

        Goto                {}


                      B:              || Cabinet:  3/3

Find any specified word or phrase - in any type of frame
```

Fig. 5.3 **Print** and **Format** options

```
Apps  Disk  Create  Edit  Locate  Frames  Words  Numbers  Graph  Print  10:43 am

                                                  Begin
                                                  Stop
                                                  Eject Page
                                              --  Pause
                                              --  Wait for Each Page

                                                  Template                        {}
                                                  Format Options
    Print Appearance ===== Headers =====             ========= Footers =========
   Offset from Left   {10}  Left                   {}  Left                      {}
   Lines per Page     {66}  Center                 {}  Center                    {}
   Spacing             {1}  Right                  {}  Right                     {}
   Width of Line      {65}  Down from Page Top {3} {3}  Up from Page Bottom  {3}
                            Start on Page      {1} {1}  Start on Page        {1}
   Condensed Print     --
   Quality Print       --   Top Margin         {6} {6}  Bottom Margin        {6}

                        B:                          Cabinet:  3/3

Specify characters between the left edge of the page and the left margin settings
```

80

Fig. 5.4 **Outline** *option*

Apps Disk Create Edit Locate Frames Words Numbers Graph Print 10:48 am

<Library>

Outline
Empty / Word Frame

<A:>
<B:>

Spreadsheet
Database
Width (£ Cols/Fields)   {50}
Height (£ Rows/Records) {100}

Columns/Fields: Add   {1}
Rows / Records: Add   {1}

Macro / Abbreviation

[   ]

B: || Cabinet: 3/3

Create an outline of nested frames

A very useful feature offered by Framework (although it is not alone in this) is the ability to create an "outline" of a set of documents. This provides you with *a ready-made skeleton for a report*, by presenting you with a number of empty "frames" which are already numbered for you. You select "**Outline**" from the "**Create**" menu, shown in Figure 5.4, when you just get a blank frame with the numbers of the sections already provided for you

1
      1.1
      1.2
      1.3
2
      2.1
      2.2
      2.3
3
      3.1
      3.2
      3.3

You can then fill in the names of the sections on the outline so that it looks as shown in Figure 5.5.

The next move is to enter one of the frames; the details are not going to be discussed here but it is very simple to do, and then you can start typing in the text of that part of the report. This is shown as it appears on the screen in Figure 5.6. Then the report can be printed out, and it will appear with the headings and numbers as shown in Figure 5.7. You should notice that the section names for the parts yet to be written are printed and await your entry, which has been completed for Section 1.1 in the example. Thus when all the sections have been typed in, each in their separate "frames", the whole document can be printed by a single command, laid out and paged for you by the program.

82

Fig. 5.5 *Filling in the outline - section names*

```
Apps  Disk  Create  Edit  Locate  Frames  Words  Numbers  Graph  Print  10:58 am

                                                                <Library>

                                                                           <A:>
                                                                           <B:>
┌[REPORT]══════════════════════════════════════════════════════════════════╗
║   1  Company Report                                                        ║
║        1.1  UK Operation                                                   ║
║        1.2  Far East Operation                                            ║
║        1.3  USA Operation                                                  ║
║   2  Financial Report                                                      ║
║        2.1  Profit and Loss                                               ║
║        2.2  Balance Sheet                                                  ║
║   3  The Products                                                          ║
║        3.1  Research & Development                                         ║
║        3.2  General Electronics                                           ║
║        3.3  Customized Systems                                            ║
╚═══════════════════════════════════════════════════════════════════════════╝

                                                                          [REPORT]

                            REPORT  │  Doc:           1/1
```

83

Fig. 5.6 *Filling in the outline - entering detail in a frame*

Apps Disk Create Edit Locate Frames Words Numbers Graph Print 11:11 am

⟨Library⟩

⟨A:⟩
⟨B:⟩

[REPORT]
[1 Company Report]
[1.1 UK Operation]
YOUR COMPANY'S OPERATION IN THE UNITED KINGDOM

In the United Kingdom your company has made considerable strides
in the past financial year. The market share has risen from
12.5% in 1986 to 15.75% in 1987. The sales force has had to be
increased from 12 salespersons to 15 salespersons and the
recruitment of a further 3 is envisaged for the forthcoming
year. Your directors are pleased to report that the introduction
of the new System 2000 home protection burglar alarm has been
met with very favourable press reports and a recent market survey
has shown that we are making a considerable market penetration in

Company Report.UK Operation Char: 66/11

Fig. 5.7 *Printing the report*

1 Company Report

1.1 UK Operation

YOUR COMPANY'S OPERATIONS IN THE UNITED KINGDOM

In the United Kingdom your company has made considerable strides in the
past financial year. The market share has risen from 12.5% in 1986 to
15.75% in 1987. The sales force has had to be increased from 12
salespersons to 15 salespersons and the recruitment of a further 3 is
envisaged for the forthcoming year. Your directors are pleased to
report that the introduction of the new System 2000 home protection
burglar alarm has been met with very favourable press reports and a
recent market survey has shown that we are making a considerable market
penetration in rural areas where, traditionally, customer resistance
has been high for products such as ours.

1.2 Far East Operation

1.3 USA Operation

2 Financial Report

2.1 Profit and loss

2.2 Balance Sheet

3 The Products

3.1 Research & Development

3.2 General Electronics

3.3 Customized systems

5.2 COMMUNICATING WITH OTHER PROGRAMS

If you do not have a program such as Framework or
Symphony then there are other ways of incorporating the
output from other programs into a word processing
document. It is all to do with what are called "ASCII"
- pronounced "Askey" - codes. ASCII stands for American
Standard Code for Information Interchange, which is a
universal standard by which each character on the
keyboard is given a numerical code which actually
reflects the *internal computer code for storage of the
character.* For example, the code produced by pressing

the **Escape** key is given the ASCII code 27, "**A**" is 65 and "**a**" is 97. As this is a universal code understood by all microcomputers it is possible to pass information between computers and between documents created by different programs on the same computer.

When a word processor, such as WordStar, creates a document it embeds inside the text, as described in Section 2.1, a series of codes that cause text to be modified in some way. It also puts in special *control* characters that enable the program to keep track of pages of text and so on. This means that the pure ASCII codes of the text itself are often mixed up with other codes that are of no relevance to any other program except that particular word processor. The result of this is that if a document created by one word processor needs to be read by another then a *conversion process* has to be undergone. In this process, the redundant codes have to be stripped out before the text can be made comprehensible to another word processor.

A similar process has to take place if you have data displayed on a spreadsheet and it has to be incorporated into a document, say a report, created by a word processor. Such a situation could happen if the spreadsheet shown in Figure 5.8 has to be read into a word processor. The spreadsheet was produced by the program called SuperCalc (see Glossary). Spreadsheets can be created, saved and edited by a spreadsheet program in the same way as documents are by a word processor.

Fig 5.8 *A spreadsheet read into a word processor*

```
                    The Computer Company Ltd

Sales of PCs
                       1986        1987        1988
UK                   50,000      65,000      89,000
Europe               31,000      35,000      45,000
USA                   5,000      10,000      15,000
SE Asia               8,500      10,500      25,000
Rest of World        10,000      12,500      35,000
                   -----------------------------------
                    104,500     133,000     209,000
```

Word processors are interested only in characters and so if you wish to extract information from a file produced by another type of program then it is only the *essential characters* in the file that have to be transmitted to the word processor. This involves a conversion process which is usually quite simple to perform, provided you know what the conversion process is actually doing.

You have already seen that a word processor program places special codes within the text in order to *define the layout* of your document. Similarly, a spreadsheet program willinsertinstructions to ensure that the datait contains is lined up properly and the text, numbers and formulas are identifiable by the program. These codes have to be removed before the contents of a spreadsheet document is transmitted to the word processor. In order to do this the spreadsheet program must have the ability to write *only the data contained within the sheet* to a disk file. Such a file will usually have a **PRN** extension added to its name by the program. Thisis usually done by asking the program to send the contents of the sheet to a file rather than to your printer. Because printers accept only ASCII codes the program is "fooled" into thinking thatitis printing even though itis not. The resulting file - now containing only ASCII characters, and identified by its PRN extension - can then be read by a word processor quite easily.

In the same way, a *database file* is quite simply a collection of information - both in numeric and in alphabetic form. It might be a collection of names, addresses and details of payments into a book club, for example. Popular database programs are dBASE II, dBASE III and DELTA (see Glossary). The data is stored in special way by the database program forits own purposes. In order to make the contents of a file readable by a word processor, a spreadsheet program or even another database program the codes particular to that program have again to be removed; the usual way that the resulting data is presented to a word processor is in "Comma Separated Value" form. This means that the separate pieces of data are turned into a string of characters separated by commas. Such a file will often have a **TXT** extension denoting that it contains ASCII characters only. An example of this is shown in Figure

5.9. This figure shows part of a database of information arranged in tabular form and presented by the database program itself, dBASE III in this case. Figure 5.10 shows the data transformed ready for being read by a word processor.

Once you have the data transformed in this manner it can be used as the basis of a mailing list data file. The advantage of using this technique is that when you have a database program you can use it to select entries with certain characteristics from a file. This means that you can make selections from a very large file ofinformation and then use this information (usually names and addresses)in a word processor-based mailing list. Some word processors have this facility, but not all of them. WordStar, for example, does not.

Fig 5.9 *Database in ASCII*

Record£	SURNAME	INTITALS	TITLE	ADDRESS1	ADDR
1	Harris	JD	Mr	45 High Street	Bale
2	Keen	PLJ	Mrs	87 Watling Street	Harr
3	French	P	Mr	The Grove	Wind
4	Hart	MP	Ms	Flat 3, The Gables	Grov
5	Lemmon	RD	Major	"Inkerman"	Well

Fig 5.10 *Database ready to be read by   word processor*

```
"Harris","JD","Mr","45 High Street","Baledon, Cambs","C84 6TY",34.50
"Keen","PLJ","Mrs","87 Watling Street","Harriden, Lincs","LC7 9KL",20.00
"French","P","Mr","The Grove","Windlesham, Norfolk","NR5 3QQ",9.78
"Hart","MP","Ms","Flat 3, The Gables","Grove Road, Harblow","HR2 4PL",45.00
"Lemmon","RD","Major",""Inkerman"","Wellington Road","Hanbury HB4 5TW",0.00
```

DESK TOP PUBLISHING

Desk top publishing (DTP) is becoming a hot favourite for the computing breakthrough of the 1980s. It might be worthwhile, before looking at what is currently available, briefly to examine the process that has been in use for years when any printed document has been produced. This applies equally well to newspapers, books, catalogues of goods or company reports.

The first task was to produce what is usually known as the "copy" on a typewriter, in double spacing on one side of the paper and as legible as the ability of the typist can make it. This then has to be edited ready for typesetting. This process of "copy editing" consists of an experienced person deciding on the general layout of the text. The typefaces to be used, the length of the lines, the number of lines on the page and the way that the text is presented on the page is usually decided by the publisher in order to create what is known as a "style". The text has to marked up in order to conform to this style by a copy editor who includes instructions to the person who is going to set up the type regarding such things as the amount of the indent of the first character of a paragraph and the "weight" of certain characters. The weight of a character is a measure of its boldness.

Then the marked up copy is sent to the typesetter who has to key the text in again at the typesetting machine ensuring that all the instructions marked on the copy are followed. When this task is complete a set of "galley proofs" are produced. These are long strips of paper with the text printed on them. At this time no attempt is made to separate the text into pages or include any pictures or diagrams. The next move is to have the text checked by the author who marks the galley proofs whenever a mistake has been made by the type-setter.

The corrected proofs are then sent to another editor who divides the galleys up into pages and incorporates the illustrations in their correct places. This is the page make-up stage. Only then can the index be compiled since the page numbers on the author's original copy bear no relation to the final product.

At this point the printing can be started. You can see that this is all a very lengthy and complicated business. Much of it is very skilled and has to be performed, particularly the typesetting, by people who have served long apprenticeships.

The latest word processors allow a lot of the work described above to be performed by the originator of the text on a PC: hence the term "Desk Top Publishing".

6.1 USING A WORD PROCESSOR

Modern word processing programs are now so versatile that many of them include features that are half way towards those required by a desk top publishing system. One of these features is the ability to produce text in *two or more columns*. What is more, these columns often need to "snake" or behave like newspaper columns. This means that you read down the first column and when you reach the bottom you return to the top of the next column in order to continue. An example of this is shown in Figure 6.1, which has taken the first part of this chapter and printed it in two parallel columns just as in a newspaper. The text is right justified but if you look carefully you will see that the result is not quite perfect. The printer has not been able to cope with the word "incorporates" towards the bottom of the right hand column. Because there are only four words on that line, due to the pitch that has been chosen, the printer cannot fit everything in properly and so the last letter of the word hangs over the edge and looks unsightly. The line needs editing manually and a hyphen inserted. The result, which looks a lot better, is in Figure 6.2.

You should also notice that the chapter heading and sub-heading are in a bolder font in order to give a more professional look to the work. Figure 6.3 shows the same text displayed in three newspaper type columns. The

90

space between the columns is known in the printing
industry as a "gutter" and can be changed as you wish.

Fig 6.1 *Newspaper 2-column layout*

CHAPTER 6

DESK TOP PUBLISHING

Desk top publishing (DTP) is becoming a hot favourite for the computing breakthrough of the nineteen eighties. It might be worthwhile, before looking at what is currently available, briefly to examine the process that has been in use for years when any printed document has been produced. This applies equally well to newpapers, books, catalogues of goods or company reports.

The first task was to produce what is usually known as the "copy" on a typewriter, in double spacing on one side of the paper and as legible as the ability of the typist can make it. This then has to be edited ready for typesetting. This process of "copy editing" consists of an experienced person deciding on the general layout of the text. The typefaces to be used, the length of the lines, the number of lines on the page and the way that the text is presented on the page is usually decided by the publisher in order to create what is known as a "house style". The text has to marked-up in order to conform to this house style by a copy editor by including instructions to the person who is going to set up the type regarding such things as the amount of the indent of the first character of a paragraph

and the "weight" of certain characters. The weight of a character is a measure of its boldness.

Then the marked up copy is sent to the typesetter who has to key the text in again at the typesetting machine ensuring that all the instructions marked on the copy are followed. When this task is complete a set of "galley proofs" are produced. These are long strips of paper with the text printed on them. At this time no attempt is made to separate the text into pages or include any pictures or diagrams. The next move is to have the text checked by the author who marks the galley proofs whenever a mistake has been made by the typesetter.

The corrected proofs are then sent to another editor who divides the galleys up into pages and incorporates the illustrations in their correct places. This is the page make-up stage. Only then can the index be compiled since the page numbers on the author's original copy bear no relation to the final product.

At this point the printing can be started. You can see that this is all a very lengthy and complicated business. Much of it is very skilled and has to be performed, particularly the typesetting,

Fig 6.2 *Editing 2-column text*

CHAPTER 6

DESK TOP PUBLISHING

Desk top publishing (DTP) is becoming a hot favourite for the computing breakthrough of the nineteen eighties. It might be worthwhile, before looking at what is currently available, briefly to examine the process that has been in use for years when any printed document has been produced. This applies equally well to newpapers, books, catalogues of goods or company reports.

The first task was to produce what is usually known as the "copy" on a typewriter, in double spacing on one side of the paper and as legible as the ability of the typist can make it. This then has to be edited ready for typesetting. This process of "copy editing" consists of an experienced person deciding on the general layout of the text. The typefaces to be used, the length of the lines, the number of lines on the page and the way that the text is presented on the page is usually decided by the publisher in order to create what is known as a "house style". The text has to marked-up in order to conform to this house style by a copy editor by including instructions to the person who is going to set up the type regarding such things as the amount of the indent of the first character of a paragraph and the "weight" of certain characters. The weight of a character is a measure of its boldness.

Then the marked up copy is sent to the typesetter who has to key the text in again at the typesetting machine ensuring that all the instructions marked on the copy are followed. When this task is complete a set of "galley proofs" are produced. These are long strips of paper with the text printed on them. At this time no attempt is made to separate the text into pages or include any pictures of diagrams. The next move is to have the text checked by the author who marks the galley proofs whenever a mistake has been made by the typesetter.

The corrected proofs are then sent to another editor who divides the galleys up into pages and incorporates the illustrations in their correct places. This is the page make-up stage. Only then can the index be compiled since the page numbers on the author's original copy bear no relation to the final product.

At this point the printing can be started. You can see that this is all a very lengthy and complicated business. Much of it is very skilled and has to be performed, particularly the typesetting,

The trouble with using a word processor to produce this type of text is that what you see on the screen is not always what you see when printed. Although you can see characters emboldened and underlined on the screen (a frequent requirement in day-to-day word processing) the commonly used word processors do not have the ability to display anything more than that. Special characters or different fonts are not usually displayed on the screen. This is because every character you see on a screen is actually "drawn" by a piece of computer software included in the operating system. The ability to draw larger and more varied types of characters on the screen usually needs additional software.

In order to have more than the usual sets of characters displayed by whatever program you are using you need first of all to send the computer into "graphics" mode. Have you noticed that the screen displays characters in the same typeface whether you are using a word processor or not? If you look closely at the screen of your PC you will see that each character is made from a matrix of dots, eight vertically and five horizontally. The five horizontal dots are so close together that they blur into a line. This severely restricts the choice of characters displayed on the screen. The only way to overcome this problem is to run the screen in a higher definition mode, in order to make it possible to draw a larger range of characters by increasing the number of dots per character. This means you need special electronics to do it. Then the characters can be "drawn" in almost any position on the screen so that proportional spacing can take place. This means that you are then able to see exactly what you are going get finally on paper.

Even the sets of characters (although much greater variety than screen-generated ones) provided by a good dot matrix printer are not really sufficient to produce an end product comparable with that produced by a human typesetter with thousands of fonts to draw on however, we can go quite a long way towards this end as you will see.

Fig 6.3 *3-column layout*

CHAPTER 6

DESK TOP PUBLISHING

Desk top publishing (DTP) is becoming a hot favourite for the computing breakthrough of the nineteen eighties. It might be worthwhile, before looking at what is currently available, briefly to examine the process that has been in use for years when any printed document has been produced. This applies equally well to newpapers, books, catalogues of goods or company reports.

The first task was to produce what is usually known as the "copy" on a typewriter, in double spacing on one side of the paper and as legible as the ability of the typist can make it. This then has to be edited ready for typesetting. This process of "copy editing" consists of an experienced person deciding on the general layout of the text. The typefaces to be used, the length of the lines, the number of lines on the page and the way that the text is presented on the page is usually decided by the publisher in order to create what is known as a "house style". The text has to marked-up in order to conform to this house style by a copy editor by including instructions to the person who is going to set up the type regarding such things as the amount of the indent of the first character of a paragraph and the "weight" of certain characters. The weight of a character is a measure of its boldness.

Then the marked up copy is sent to the typesetter who has to key the text in again at the typesetting machine ensuring that all the instructions marked on the copy are followed. When this task is complete a set of "galley proofs" are produced. These are long strips of paper with the text printed on them. At this time no attempt is made to separate the text into pages or include any pictures of diagrams. The next move is to have the text checked by the author who marks the galley proofs whenever a mistake has been made by the typesetter.

The corrected proofs are then sent to another editor who divides the galleys up into pages and incorporates the illustrations in their correct places. This is the page make-up stage. Only then can the index be compiled since the page numbers on the author's original copy bear no relation to the final product.

At this point the printing can be started. You can see that this is all a very lengthy and complicated business. Much of it is very skilled and has to be performed, particularly the typesetting, by people who served long apprenticeships.

The latest word processors allow a lot of the work described above to be performed by

Fig 6.4 *Adjusting the text to accommodate illustrations*

When a conventional mechanical typewriter is being used the typist has control over the appearance of the right hand end of each line of type. Decisions can be made as to whether the last word of the line is to be hyphenated or a space left at the end of the line with the word typed at the start of the next line. The result is a "ragged" right hand margin. If a piece of text in a book or a newspaper is set by hand, not a very common practice these days, the compositor or typesetter is able to insert small spacers between the words in order to provide a clean right hand margin. This operation produces what is called "right justified text". It is a very skilled operation and is only possible on a typewriter if the number of letters in each line is counted and the typist puts the spaces in as each line is typed. The final result takes a lot of time, but the appearance of the finished text is very much enhanced.

With a word processor we can leave the task of counting the letters and words and inserting the correct number of spaces for us if required. The problem is however, not a simple as that. Compare the two identical pieces of text shown in Figures 3.1 and 3.2. The first of these shows the text printed with no justification and the second shows it right justified. Notice particularly the unsightly extra spaces in the second

line. These are there because the program knows how many characters there

space for

Figure 3.1

are to be in a line and that the first word on the third line is too long to be included in the line above and so the thirteen spaces left over – there has to be at least one between each

space for

Figure 3.2

word – are inserted reasonably evenly between the seven words on that line. You might also notice that the words themselves can look strange because each letter is allowed to take up the same character width. But an "i" is not as wide as, for example, an "r" or an "f", so, look at the word "frightened" on the second line and you will see that the word takes up rather too much space and this is particularly noticeable when the text is justified. These irritations can be

Fig 6.4 - *Continued*

resolved as you will see in
sections 3.5 and 3.10.
A useful variation of
right hand justification is
when you wish to have a
document where although it
is not justified in the
sense described above you
have a clean right hand
edge and a clean left hand
edge as is shown in Figure
3.3. This is a similar
function to that of decimal
tabs which are covered in
the next section.

There is another restriction that a system such as this suffers from. It is because text typed in while the word processor is in column mode will "snake". This means that the first column is filled up first and when the bottom of the page is reached the cursor will jump to the head of the next column to continue the text. This means that when the document is finished there could well be half a column filled and the rest of the page left blank, as shown in the second part of Figure 6.4. In publishing circles this problem is known as "balancing" the columns. This means that when a document comes to its end the text on the last page is divided equally between the columns so that the partial columns are all of the same length. On the second page of the document shown in Figure 6.5 the columns have been balanced manually. What was done was that the number of lines on the second page were counted and then a page break inserted in the column after the eighth line. This forces the rest of the column up into the right-hand column and certainly improves the general appearance of the text.

Fig 6.5 *Manual balancing of columns*

When a conventional mechanical typewriter is being used the typist has control over the appearance of the right hand end of each line of type. Decisions can be made as to whether the last word of the line is to be hyphenated or a space left at the end of the line with the word typed at the start of the next line. The result is a 'ragged' right hand margin. If a piece of text in a book or a newspaper is set by hand, not a very common practice these days, the compositor or typesetter is able to insert small spacers between the words in order to provide a clean right hand margin. This operation produces what is called 'right justified text'. It is a very skilled operation and is only possible on a typewriter if the number of letters in each line is counted and the typist puts the spaces in as each line is typed. The final result takes a lot of time, but the appearance of the finished text is very much enhanced.

With a word processor we can leave the task of counting the letters and words and inserting the correct number of spaces for us if required. The problem is however, not a simple as that. Compare the two identical pieces of text shown in Figures 3.1 and 3.2. The first of these shows the text printed with no justification and the second shows it right justified. Notice particularly the unsightly extra spaces in the second

line. These are there because the program knows how many characters there

space for

Figure 3.1

are to be in a line and that the first word on the third line is too long to be included in the line above and so the thirteen spaces left over – there has to be at least one between each

space for

Figure 3.2

word – are inserted reasonably evenly between the seven words on that line. You might also notice that the words themselves can look strange because each letter is allowed to take up the same character width. But an 'i' is not as wide as, for example, an 'r' or an 'f', so, look at the word 'frightened' on the second line and you will see that the word takes up rather too much space and this is particularly noticeable when the text is justified. These irritations can be

Fig 6.5 - *Continued*

resolved as you will see in sections 3.5 and 3.10.

A useful variation of right hand justification is when you wish to have a document where although it is not justified in the sense described above you have a clean right hand edge and a clean left hand edge as is shown in Figure 3.3. This is a similar function to that of decimal tabs which are covered in the next section.

6.2 USING SECOND GENERATION WORD PROCESSORS

Now a new generation of word processors is coming on the market. They are often marketed as Desk Top Publishing systems, but they are really very sophisticated word processors. They have all the features of conventional word processors but in addition they have the facility to display a *range of typefaces* on the screen, include *illustrations* such as photographs and drawings in with the text and *store them all on disk*. You can also change the size of sections of the text so that a proper professional-looking page make up can be achieved.

The majority of these systems work in conjunction with a *graphics system* such as Windows or GEM (Graphics Environment Manager - See Glossary). The way in which such a system is used falls into four stages. Firstly, all the parts of the publication - whether it be a newspaper, advertising handout or report - are *stored on disk*. The copy - i.e. the text to be printed - is typed as with any conventional word processor. Any illustrations to be included in the text can be stored on disk by feeding them through a scanning device that "digitises" them. This is the technique of coding each tiny section of the picture so that its intensity and colour can be represented by a number. This number is stored on the disk and the reverse procedure will recombine the picture ready for display in the screen or printing (it is a similar system to that used to record music on a compact disc).

Having made sure that all the copy and illustrations

are safely stored away you can define what is often called the "style" of the document. This is the definition of the *layout of the page*. This includes, among other things, the position of the margins, the number of columns and their width and the fonts you wish to use for headings.

The next stage is to start making the pages up one at a time by retrieving the text and illustrations one at a time from disk and placing them on the page. As you do this you can change the size of any of the illustrations, or crop them (cut borders from them) and move them about until you have satisfied yourself that everything looks exactly as you want it. A typical piece of software that allows you to achieve this is PageMaker (see Glossary). It works in conjunction with the Windows graphics package and a mouse. The term "mouse" in a computing context is used for a device that is connected to the system box. It consists of a ball protruding through the bottom of a hand-held device that rolls over a flat surface. The movement of the mouse is reflected in the movement of a point across your screen. Two buttons on the top of the mouse allow you mark a point on the screen by "clicking" the mouse. A mouse is shown in Figure 6.6.

Once you are satisfied with the layout you can print the document page by page on a laser printer. This produces what is called "camera ready copy", which is ready for photographing in order to produce the final plates from which the document is to be printed.

Fig 6.6 *A mouse*

6.3 **TYPESETTING**

The long history of printing has caused a number of terms from the early days of printing to be perpetuated in the newer technology. Terms such as "leading" and "picas" are still used today even though the hot-metal printing process is now to all intents and purposes long dead.

First of all a few definitions; the "set" of a letter is its *width*, the "body" of a typeface is its *depth.* The set and the body are measured in a unit called a "point" which is 0.01383 inches, approximately one seventy-second of an inch. The point is the fundamental unit of *typographical measurement.* A "pica" (it rhymes with "biker") is twelve points and is one-sixth of an inch. Measurements across a page are made in picas. *Spaces* are measured in "ems" or "ens" so that you have what are called "en-spaces" and "em-spaces". An en-space is the space left between words and is half as wide as its depth. An em-space is a space where its width is equal to its body size.

The width of the page is called its "measure" and is measured in picas. The depth of a page can be measured in lines. However, because there is a need to have each line separated from its fellow, there was traditionally a strip of lead used to separate lines and the width of this lead was measured in points. Hence the depth of a page is sometimes known as the "leading" (rhymes with "bedding") and will be measured in points.

For simplicity we could divide typefaces into two types, Roman and italic, *this being in italics.* There are, in fact, many more, but all types have upper case for capital letters, known as "caps" by the printer, and lower case letters. The various typefaces (or *fonts*) are known by a generic name and their size in points. Fonts come in families each member having design features in common, their difference in size being denoted by the number of points making up the body of the font. We therefore get 6-point Times Bold, 8-point Times Bold, up to 14-point Times Bold. Figure 6.7 illustrates some of the most popular fonts and typefaces.

Fig 6.7 *Some popular fonts and typefaces*

14	**Helv Bold**	**ABCDEFGHIJ**
12	Courier	ABCDEFGHIJKLM
12	Courier Landscape	ⱯᗺƆᗡƎℲ⅁ Η
12	**Courier Bold**	**ABCDEFGHIJKLM**
12	*Courier Italic*	*ABCDEFGHIJKLM.*
10	Tms Roman	ABCDEFGHIJKLN
10	**Tms Roman Bold**	**ABCDEFGHIJKLN**
10	*Tms Roman Italic*	*ABCDEFGHIJKLM*
10	Tms Roman Comp.	ABCDEFGHIJKLMN
10	**Tms Roman Comp. Bold**	**ABCDEFGHIJKLMN**
10	*Tms Roman Comp. Italic*	*ABCDEFGHIJKLMN*
8	Tms Roman	ABCDEFGHIJKLMNabc
8	Tms Roman Comp.	ABCDEFGHIJKLMNabcd
8	Line Printer	ABCDEFGHIJKLMNabcdefgh
8	Line Printer Landscape	ⱯᗺƆᗡƎℲ⅁Η Ʉ.

If you have a laser printer you can use a large range of type designs, but you usually have to buy them as pieces of software, probably in the form of ROM (Read Only Memory) chips in a removable cartridge which slots into the machine when you want to use them.

When producing the finished document you have the choice of printing directly onto a laser printer. The paper that comes out of that can then be photographed and a plate made for the final printing. Alternatively you can send the output to a Linotronic (see Glossary) phototypesetting machine. Such a machine is able to produce a wider range of typefaces than the average laser printer, but is considerably more expensive.

LAPTOPS

AND

COMMUNICATIONS

With the constant improvement in technology we are now seeing many changes in what we have come to accept as "conventional" word processing. In the early days word processors were bulky machines and dedicated solely to the one task. Now we have PCs in abundance that can run programs to handle accounts, draw graphs, make financial projections and then incorporate the results from these programs into word processed documents. All this can be done by one small machine sitting on a desk.

Two recent advances give you the freedom to *take your computing power with you* wherever you have to leave the confines of your office. The first is the appearance on the scene of the small, portable, "lap top" computer. Coupled with this is the general improvement in communications both locally and internationally.

A lap top computer is a truly portable microcomputer, usually weighing in at about twelve pounds, with all the computing power of the desk top PC contained in a compact case about the size of a portable typewriter.

A typical lap top microcomputer, as shown in Figure 7.1, has no bulky television type screen. Instead this is replaced by a flat screen that works in a completely different manner. The characters on the screen are formed by what is called a "Liquid Crystal Display" (LCD for short) and although the quality is not so good at the present time as the Visual Display Unit (VDU) on a PC, it is perfectly adequate for word processing. The problem with such screens is that they are "directional" in that you have to view them at the correct angle or you will not see anything at all.

Fig 7.1 *A lap top computer*

Because no PC consumes much in the way of electrical power it is very simple to drive a lap top machine from low-voltage batteries; most of them have their own rechargeable internal battery pack. When connected to the mains supply, these batteries are recharged while the machine is in use. Another contribution to the compact size of the latest in this type of PC is the use of the smaller $3^1/_2$ inch floppy disks rather than the more common $5^1/_4$ inch disks. Surprisingly enough, these smaller disks have about *twice the storage capacity* of their larger brothers, a feature which adds to their attractiveness.

Because the small overall size of lap top PCs they do suffer from the disadvantage of having keyboards that are rather cramped to use, being reduced in overall size from the desk top machines. This often means that the actual keys are smaller and closer together and that many of the them can serve several purposes. However, there is an advantage in that the keyboard is often detachable and being light in weight can rest on your knee while the rest of the machine can sit on the tray on the back of the airline seat in front of you. Lap top PCs save you having to take your secretary with you on foreign trips and can sit on your knee without causing you to receive any funny looks!

Once you have reached your destination you can plug your lap top PC into the mains to recharge its batteries and connect it to a telephone in order to send your notes and memos back to the office.

In order to communicate with other PCs by using the telephone you need to connect your machine to the telephone network via a *modem*. A modem is the electronic device that converts the signals that come out the socket marked 'Serial' at the back of the machine into signals that can be sent over a telephone line. The modem (MOdulator DEModulator) can often be incorporated into the system box of a PC. In order to use the system you can either dial the number of your office where there must be a PC fitted with the same type of equipment which will be activated when it receives your call. Suitable software, and there is a wide selection of this about, enables a document stored on a disk on your machine to be sent over the international telephone network (and by satellite if need be) to its destination where a copy of it will be stored on a disk on the receiving machine. As the communication is two-way, messages can be sent in *both directions*.

The type of data transmission described above provides a rather better type of service than the Telex system which will only send *messages* across the world. "Direct data communications" using modems sends not only the message but also the *format* of the document. This means that you can create a document using WordPerfect in Dubai, for example, and it can then be sent using a modem via a normal telephone call to a machine in England. Assuming the machine receiving the document also has the WordPerfect word processor it can print the document out just as if it had been created on the spot.

This is not the only way that messages and documents can be transmitted over long distances. There is the International Teletex system which is similar to the Telex system but allows one word processor to send a message or a document to another word processor. Again this is an improvement over Telex as *formatted docu-*

ments, such as contracts or quotations, can be transmitted, rather than simple textual messages.

On a smaller scale there are systems that allow a number of word processing stations to be connected via a *Local Area Network* (LAN). This provides a number of separate workstations that are not full blown PCs to be connected to a central computer that contains the word processing program and all the document files. This central device is known as a "file server" and each user can have a cut-down PC - perhaps with no disk drives of its own, and without a printer. There would be a central fast, high quality printer that is used by everybody. This is a good argument for having one laser printer rather than a number of cheaper printers scattered about. The various workstations connected in a LAN can send documents to each other. This means that a secretary in one part of a building can create a document (a report for example) and send it via the network to the PC of the person who originated the report to be edited. Once any corrections have been made to the document it can then be distributed via the network to the people it is intended for. This is the basis of what is known as "electronic mail".

There is even one system that provides the sort of facilities described just now that in addition has a telephone hand set fixed to the keyboard. By using this the operator can, when a convenient place in the document is reached, lift the hand set and speak into it recording a spoken message as part of the document. It might be that the author may want a special piece of research doing where the result has to be incorporated in the document. This message is saved away with the rest of the document and when it is recalled to the screen for editing a symbol is displayed on the screen when the spoken message occurs. The operator then can lift the hand set and hear the message at that point.

Another feature of this type of system is that it provides a "mailbox" facility. This means that a secretary can produce a document ready for checking by a manager, for example. The system can store this in such a way that when the manager switches on his terminal he is informed that there is a document awaiting his attention. He can then display it on the screen without any searching on his part.

This technology explosion is certain to lead to profound changes in people's work patterns. It is no longer necessary for an executive to visit the office every day. It is not a wild guess to suggest that it will not be very long before the Sales Manager, for example, has a PC at home that he connects to his office each morning for the morning mail to be received by him over the telephone line and displayed on his screen. The sending of documents pictorially is the basis of the *Fax* system of communication now in current use. A device called a "scanner" will read a document and the document can then be transmitted to a computer anywhere in the world where it can be displayed on a screen.

When the Sales Manager goes on his travels he can take his lap top PC with him and communicate with head office, from wherever he happens to be, over the telephone which may be in his car, on a train, possibly even on an aeroplane and in a hotel room in Singapore. By this means "hard copy" - i.e., documents - can be transmitted across the world very quickly and at low cost. One person who uses this type of system in action is the author who lives in Wales and creates her television scripts on a word processor and sends them through the international telephone network to America for editing and distribution.

SUMMARY

1. A *lap top computer* is a lightweight, portable PC that is compatible with the desktop models.

2. A lap top computer runs from *internal batteries or from the mains.*

3. A *modem* is a device that allows you to connect your PC to a telephone and send documents to a PC that is similarly equipped.

4. A *local area network* (LAN) is a means of connecting a number of PCs together so that they can share a common printer and send documents electronically through the network to each other.

5. A device called a *scanner* can "read" a document and store it on disk. This saves someone having to retype the document on a word processor before it can be saved.

6. The international *Teletex* system enables documents to be transmitted all over the world between wordprocessors.

HOW TO DO . . .

8.1 A LETTER

Figure 8.1.a illustrates a typical letter that would be printed on company letterhead.
Figure 8.1.b illustrates how the same text would look if it were not justified.
Figure 8.1.c illustrates how the same letter would look if the margins were narrowed.

WHAT TO CONSIDER:

1. How to set *margins*.

2. How to select *justification* or *ragged right margins*.

3. *Insertion* and *deletion* of text.

4. *Save* operations.

5. *Print* operations.

6. *Retrieve* operations.

Fig 8.1a *Processing a letter - justified*

12 December 1988

Mrs F Greensleeves
Personnel Officer
Grays Trading Company Ltd
Grays House
High Street
Litton LT3 7AH

Dear Mrs Greensleeves

Further to your advertisement in last Thursday's
Daily Rag I would like to apply for the position of
Invoice Clerk. I have been working in a similar
capacity for three years now and would be pleased
to find work in such a reputable company as yours.

My curriculum vitae is enclosed for your
information. I hope that you will find it of
interest.

Thank you for your attention. I look forward to
hearing from you in the near future.

Yours sincerely

Georgina Lloyd

Enc.

Fig 8.1b *Processing a letter - unjustified*

12 December 1988

Mrs F Greensleeves
Personnel Officer
Grays Trading Company Ltd
Grays House
High Street
Litton LT3 7AH

Dear Mrs Greensleeves

Further to your advertisement in last Thursday's
Daily Rag I would like to apply for the position of
Invoice Clerk. I have been working in a similar
capacity for three years now and would be pleased
to find work in such a reputable company as yours.

My curriculum vitae is enclosed for your
information. I hope that you will find it of
interest.

Thank you for your attention. I look forward to
hearing from you in the near future.

Yours sincerely

Georgina Lloyd

Enc.

Fig 8.1c *Processing a letter - narrow margins*

12 December 1988

Mrs F Greensleeves
Personnel Officer
Grays Trading Company Ltd
Grays House
High Street
Litton

Dear Mrs Greensleeves

Further to your advertisement in last
Thursday's <u>Daily Rag</u> I would like to
apply for the position of Invoice Clerk.
I have been working in a similar capacity
for three years now and would be pleased
to find work in such a reputable company
as yours.

My curriculum vitae is enclosed for your
information. I hope that you will find it
of interest.

Thank you for your attention. I look
forward to hearing from you in the near
future.

Yours sincerely

Georgina Lloyd

Enc.

8.2 **A MEMO**

Figure 8.2 illustrates a typical memo

WHAT TO CONSIDER:

1. How to set *margins*.

2. How to set and clear *tabs*. Tabs are needed at the S of "Sales Managers"; at the F of "From"; at the J of "John". A *decimal tab* is needed for the figures column.

3. How to *draw a line* if you do not have pre-printed memo stationery.

4. How to *centre* "MEMORANDUM" if you do not have pre-printed memo stationery.

5. *Save* operations.

6. *Print* operations.

7. *Retrieve* operations.

Fig 8.2 *Processing a memorandum*

MEMORANDUM

To: Sales Managers   From: John Wright

Date: 1 April 1988   Subject: Monthly Target

===

I was disappointed with the March sales figures. This month
no-one reached their target. As a result I am forced to
insist that the following targets must be met for April:

Kevin Clarke   10
Lyn James   8
Robbie Burns   2
Sue Thornber   6
Julia Walker   11

As an incentive we shall be giving a magnum of champagne to
those of you who reach target this month in addition to the
usual bonus and commission.

Regards

John

8.3   AN INVOICE

Figure 8.3 illustrates a typical invoice to be printed on company notepaper/invoice stationery.

WHAT TO CONSIDER:

1. How to set *margins*.

2. How to set and clear *tabs*. A tab is needed for the "goods" and a *decimal tab* for the numbers.

3. How to *centre* "INVOICE" and the VAT No.

4. If your stationery is pre-printed for invoices you will have to make sure that the *numbers print out in the right place*. Have a trial run on plain paper first of all. When you have got it right make a note of the columns you have used. (Perhaps you could create a macro to do this for you.)

5. If your word processor can do *calculations* you could use it for the addition and calculation of the VAT.

6. *Underlining* is needed for some of the numbers.

7. *Save* operations.

8. *Print* operations.

9. *Retrieve* operations.

Fig 8.3 *Processing an invoice*

Invoice No: 12345

Date: 4 June 1988

ACCOUNTS DEPARTMENT
Park Electricals Plc
Industrial Estate
Scranton
Leics LE4 3RR

INVOICE

To:	Monthly fee for public relations work, as agreed	£1500.00
	Artwork and printing of brochure	£3155.00
	Advertisement for recruitment purposes	£500.00
	10 hours @ £60.00 (interviewing and selection)	£600.00
	SUBTOTAL	£5755.00
	VAT @ 15%	£863.25
	TOTAL	£6618.25

VAT Registered No: 888 666 888

8.4   A PRICE LIST

Figure 8.4 illustrates a price list that could be entered by your word processor and updated when required.

WHAT TO CONSIDER:

1. How to set *margins* - they will be much wider for landscape paper (portrait is A4 paper with the shorter edge downward, while landscape is A4 paper with the longer edge downward).

2. How to set *tabs* and *decimal tabs*.

3. *Continual underlining* for the title.

4. *Calculations for* the discounted price (not available with most word processors).

5. Positioning the paper in the printer for *landscape*.

116

Fig 8.4 *Processing a price list*

GOODS	QUANTITY	UNIT PRICE	DISC ON GROSS	COST OF GROSS	DATE OF PURCHASE
Tring	2400	.87	15%	£106.49	01.01.85
Wigget	1400	1.00	10%	£129.60	04.01.85
Blurb	144	5.50	10%	£712.80	16.02.85
Plunket	3000	.77	25%	£83.16	21.02.85
Hunk	1440	.99	21%	£112.62	03.03.85
Graballe	288	15.00	12%	£1900.08	31.03.85

Figure 8.4

8.5   A QUOTATION

Figure 8.5a illustrates a typical company quotation
where the main text for the document has been stored as
standard paragraphs or glossaries which are retrieved as
required. You should always remember that a word
processor *helps you avoid repetitive work*.
Figure 8.5b illustrates the standard document that you
will create and save. Each time you send out a quotation
retrieve this file into a new document and fill in the
gaps. You could use *stop codes* to move the cursor
directly to the location of the variable information.

WHAT TO CONSIDER:

1. How to set *margins*.

2. How to set *tabs* for the text and a *dec tab* for
   the amount. Store the settings (ruler line or
   equivalent) with the mask document.

3. How to use *stop codes* if your system has this
   option.

4. *Save* operations.

Fig 8.5a *Processing a company quotation*

QUOTATION

for

LORD JILLINGHAM

Event:	Medieval Banquet	
Number of Guests:	150	
Location:	Crackle Hall, Rootland	
Date:	24th January 1988	
Time:	19.30 - 02.30	

Aperitif:	Mulled wine with cloves	£ 150.00
Potage:	Venison and mulberry	£ 320.00
Hors d'oeuvre	Brawn of hock with soda bread	£ 300.00
Main course:	Rack of pink English lamb with rosemary	£ 600.00
Cheese:	Stilton with grapes	£ 75.00
Dessert:	Syllabub	£ 270.00
Beverages:	Ale and mead	£ 300.00

TOTAL: £ 2015.00

PRICE PER HEAD £ 13.43

Use Society Caterers of Bath for a time to remember. Our quoted prices are exclusive of VAT and 12% service charge. Staff and equipment are supplied at no extra cost.

Table linen, floral arrangements and entertainment can be provided if required.

Fig 8.5b *Standard quotation document*

QUOTATION

for

Event:
Number of Guests:
Location:
Date:

Time:

Aperitif:
Potage:
Hors d'oeuvre:
Main course:
Cheese:
Dessert:
Beverages:

TOTAL:

PRICE PER HEAD

Figure 8.5c illustrates the extra standard paragraphs that could then be retrieved at the end of the file according to the requirements of the quotation.

WHAT TO CONSIDER:

1. How to set the margins so that they are the same as for the *body of the text*.

2. How to create, save and recall *standard paragraphs*.

3. How to enter variable information into a standard paragraph - perhaps using *stop codes* or *markers*.

4. *Save* operations.

Fig 8.5c *Extra standard paragraphs for quotation*

PARA1

Use Society Caterers of Bath for a time to remember. Our quoted prices are exclusive of VAT and 12% service charge. Staff and equipment are supplied at no extra cost.

PARA2

Use Society Caterers of Bath for all your office parties. We specialise in theme nights. Please telephone for our brochure.

PARA3

Our prices are quoted exclusive of VAT. No service charge will be made at a charity event. Any tips received will be donated to the charity.

PARA4

Table linen, floral arrangements and entertainment can be provided if required.

8.6   A REPORT

Figure 8.6 illustrates the first four pages of a company report. Whenever you start a long report it is vital to set the *format parameters* before you start. Once this is done the rest should be plain sailing. Some word processors have facilities for repagination, this will help you to create pages of uniform length automatically. A widow and orphan facility will make sure that you never find the last line of a paragraph at the top of a page or the first line of a paragraph at the bottom of a page.

Reports are notorious for being altered. Paragraphs may be moved, text deleted and large chunks inserted. With a word processor many of these changes can be done simply and   efficiently.

WHAT TO CONSIDER:

1.   How to set *margins*.

2.   How to set a *tab* for the indented text.

3.   *Automatic section numbering* (often called outlining) could be useful.

4.   How to set *footnotes* (if available with your program).

5.   How to *underline* (and how to *remove underline*).

6.   How to *embolden* (and how to *remove bold*).

7.   How to set a *header* that runs across the top of all but the first page.

8.   How to set a *footer* that runs across the base of all but the first page.

9.   How to set an *automatic page number* in a footer.

10.   How to set and remove *page breaks*.

11. How to *disallow widows and orphans* (if available with your program).

12. How to *move* text.

13. How to *copy* text.

14. *Repagination* if you have to make a lot of alterations (if available with your program).

15. The "window" feature could be useful so that you can be reminded of the *subjects and their order* as you type.

16. How to set up the printer for *multiple pages* (hand fed, sheet fed or continuous stationery).

17. How to print *more than one copy* of a document.

18. How to use a *spelling checker*.

Fig 8.6 *Processing a report*

ANNUAL REPORT WINDMILL TRAINING SERVICES

APRIL 1988

SUBJECTS

1. Performance 87/88
2. Failings 87/88
3. Profit 87/88
4. Staff
5. The Future 87 /88

1   PERFORMANCE

1.1   MARKET

In the marketplace performance has improved. We have overtaken our arch rivals BES and seem to have about a 25% share in the market in the county. In the town itself market share has risen to almost 80%. We have established that the medium to large companies provide the most business. However the home user and small businessman should still be approached and won over. We only provided services for 10 small firms during the year.

1.2   TARGETS

With a team of 3 telesales executives the Sales Team have found it easier to reach their targets. The telesales team themselves have found it hard work. Bonuses were achieved by every salesman at least once. Each salesman should aim to reach bonus at least every other month. A minimum of 75 calls must be made each day and 5 appointments made. Extra mailshots will be supplied to make this easier. Salesmen and women "on the road" should make at least two calls a day. If the appointments have not been made by Telesales then get on the phone yourselves.

Page 1 of 4

Fig 8.6 *Processing a report - Continued*

WINDMILL TRAINING SERVICES 87/88

1.3   <u>ATTITUDE</u>

There has been a marked improvement in attitude. Confidence in the product is paramount. Remember our motto "Windmill's Need Sales".

1.4   <u>TRAINING</u>

The course questionnaires have been studied carefully. Well done everyone. They love your witty exercises Henry, and Jenny is popular with the men. I think the "Twenty Questions" sessions at the end of the course were extremely well received.

2   **FAILINGS**

2.1   <u>SALES</u>

Sales were up on last year but not enough to justify the extra staff taken on board last September. Each salesman should aim to book 10 training courses per month. The average performance was 7. Unless this improves staff numbers will be reduced.

2.2   <u>MARKETING</u>

The Marketing Department opened a year ago. Most of the year was taken up with laborious research and assessment of the market. Now it's time to get down to some hard promotion. Your budget should no longer be spent on telephone calls and mailshots. Please can we have more exhibitions and open evenings. The appointment of a PR consultancy has not yet paid off. More creative input is required.

2.3   <u>MAGAZINE</u>

You said you wanted an in-house magazine. We bought a desk top publisher. It is still not being used.

Page 2 of 4

Fig 8.6 *Processing a report - Continued*

WINDMILL TRAINING SERVICES 87/88

Marketing will take over responsibility for this publication and it will now act as a user magazine and will be issued quarterly.

3   PROFIT

Overall profit is less than in 86/87. The move to larger premises and employment of extra staff has eaten into the profit. We have broken even on our investment.

4   STAFF

4.1   HIRING

Welcome to Tim Hughes and Janice Loper.[1] The Sales Department has been a lot noisier since your arrival last September. Good luck in the future and I hope you enjoy your weekend in Paris, Tim.

Welcome also to Kelly Adams, surely you must be the shortest lived YTS student in England. We were delighted to bring you on board after just one week. We look forward to seeing you on the Board in 10 years.

John Knight joined the Accounts Department at Christmas. Welcome and try and keep us in the Black!

4.2   FIRING (well not exactly)

Goodbye to Tina Green who left us last week to have her baby. We look forward to seeing you back here in a few months.

Page 3 of 4

---

[1]Janice was married last Saturday and is now Mrs Kitson

Fig 8.6 *Processing a report - Continued*

WINDMILL TRAINING SERVICES 87/88

Henry Johnson left the Training Department to take up a position in Dubai. You are the first to leave us from Training, let's hope you are the last.

5   THE FUTURE

We will soon have a magazine for the user base which should keep the established clients coming back for more.

Expansion further afield is necessary if we are to make a good profit this year. Please can everyone promote Windmill even when off duty. After all, you all want a good Christmas bonus this year don't you?

One extra training room is being constructed behind the Board Room. This will be a teach yourself centre, designed to cater for the needs of those who cannot spare a day from work and would like to spend an hour or so per day with a good course book.

Thank you all very much for your support, I look forward to another glowing year.

Best wishes

George Stevenson
Chairman

8.7 HINTS FOR AUTHORS

Most of today's authors, including Joanna and Peter Gosling, of course, would be lost without a word processor. However, it is not just the moving, copying and deletion of text that is needed. Sophisticated word processors can take all the paper shuffling away. No longer do you need to write down index entries on scraps of paper and then put them into order; instead an index can be generated automatically, with just a little intervention from the operator. A waste paper basket piled high with frustrated balls of paper is a thing of the past.

Some sections of Macmillan's Advice to Authors are as follows:

> The material that goes to the printer must be a complete and original typescript, double spaced, on one side only of good quality paper, preferably A4 (294 x 206 mm), with ample margins. All these points seen obvious but still need emphasising...
>
> We cannot proceed with a typescript where any part of the text, e.g. a chapter, Notes and References or Bibliography, are missing. We can accept a typescript where parts of the preliminary pages or of the endmatter are still to follow, but only by special arrangement.
>
> We must have the top copy for the printer; carbon copies, duplicated material or photocopies are acceptable only for the other copies. It also helps the printer if a typewriter with a constant character width and number of lines per page are used.
>
> **Double spacing** is essential...
>
> **Margins** should be a minimum depth of 25mm at head, foot and right of the page and width 40 mm at the left. Both the copy-editor and the printer's estimator need this space for their annotations..

Number the folios of the text on the top right-hand corners. This numbering should be continued to include the endmatter, if any, but the preliminary pages should be numbered separately. We will accept a typescript where the chapters are numbered separately, especially in the case of a compilation; but it is in your own interest to number the text folios right through (folios are referred to when writing to you at the editing stage). The total number of folios in the typescript should be written on the first folio.

WHAT TO CONSIDER:

1. How to set the *default page length* and *margin size* parameters required by the publishing company.

2. How to set *double spacing*.

3. How to print in *draft mode* in order to save ribbons.

4. How to set *headers with or without page numbers.*

5. How to set *footers with or without page numbers.*

6. How to create, edit and delete *footnotes*.

7. How to create, edit and delete *endnotes*.

8. How to *disallow widows and orphans*.

9. How to use *windows* or *switch screen facilities* for reference purposes or to copy text between documents.

10. How to create *each chapter* in a *separate document* and then print them with *consecutive page numbers*.

11. How to search for two spaces between sentences in order to replace them with just *one space*.

12. How to use the *spelling checker* and create your own personal dictionaries for common terms.

13. How to use the *Thesaurus*.

14. How to back up your documents in order to *safeguard your work*.

15. How to identify text for a *table of contents* and generate it.

16. How to *display* the table of contents - i.e. with/without dot leaders, etc.

17. How to identify text for an *index* and generate it.

18. How to use the *sort facility* for index entries that were not generated by an indexing facility.

19. How to use *repagination* if your document has been altered a great deal.

20. How to alter the *pitch* and *font*.

21. How to *justify* the text or use *proportional spacing*.

22. How to set the level of *hyphenation* required.

23. How to fix any margin, tab or other format changes so that these parameters are *saved* with the document.

24. How to create and use *macros* for repetitive commands or text.

25. How to create *libraries* (glossaries) and use and re-use the entries.

26. How to *copy text* into one file from another.

27. How to *mark text* for possible rewrites.

28. How to *move the cursor quickly* around the document.

29. How to *edit* one document while *printing* another.

30. How to *send text to your publisher* via a *modem*.

31. How to produce *camera-ready copy* with the choice of fonts available in your program and a laser printer.

32. Whether your program is compatible with a *desk top publisher* at a later stage.

33. Whether the HELP facility is *context sensitive* and adequate for use in a hurry.

8.8   **A LEGAL DOCUMENT**

Figure 8.8a illustrates part of a lease document. A document such as this could be saved as a *standard paragraph* and then recalled and used for all future lease work. Stop codes should be used so that you can take the cursor quickly to the places where information is to be inserted. If your program does not have a stop code facility you could put a * or some other symbol at each location instead of a stop code and then "search" for each occurrence.
 Once the standard document has been created and saved you can create a new document and recall the standard document to use as a *mask* for the variable information. (see Figure 8.8b)

WHAT TO CONSIDER:

1. How to create a document to save and recall as a *standard paragraph*.

2. How to use stop codes or symbols to move to for the *variable information*.

3. How to *indent* text.

4. How to *underline* text.

5. How to *reform a document* once additional text has been inserted.

6. How to save the new document under a *different name* from the standard paragraph document.

Fig 8.7a *A blank lease document*

(1) T H I S L E A S E made the * day of * 198

(2) BETWEEN * of * in the County of * (hereinafter called the

Lessor which expression where the context admits includes

the persons for the time being entitled in reversion

immediately expectant on the term hereby granted) of the one

part and <u>*</u> of * in the said County of * (hereinafter called

the Lessee which expression where the context admits

includes the persons deriving title under the Lessee) of

(3) the other part WITNESSES as follows

(4) 1 THE Lessor hereby demises unto the Lessee ALL THAT

messuage and premises situate on the * side of

(5)   * in the said County of * and known as * aforesaid

hereinafter called the property

(6) TO HOLD unto the Lessee for the term of * from the   day

of   198 YIELDING

(7) AND PAYING therefor during the said term the yearly rent of

<u>*</u> (£ *) clear of all deductions (except as hereinafter

mentioned) by equal quarterly payments on the usual quarter

days in every year the first of such payments to be made on

the   day of   next

2   THE Lessee hereby covenants with the Lessor as

follows

Fig 8.7b A *completed lease document*

(1)   T H I S   L E A S E   made the 4th day of April 1989

(2)   BETWEEN MARGOT MCBRIDE of 65, The Cherry Grove, Farnham in

the County of Surrey (hereinafter called the Lessor which

expression where the context admits includes the persons for

the time being entitled in reversion immediately expectant

on the term hereby granted) of the one part and KEVIN KEEGER

of 76, Jumairah Street in the said County of Wessex

(hereinafter called the Lessee which expression where the

context admits includes the persons deriving title under the

Lessee) of

(3)   the other part WITNESSES as follows

(4)   1 THE Lessor hereby demises unto the Lessee ALL THAT

messuage and premises situate on the west side of

(5)   Geneva Square in the said County of Hampshire and known as

Top Flat, King Street aforesaid hereinafter called the property

(6)   TO HOLD unto the Lessee for the term of three years from the

4th day of April 1987 YIELDING

(7)   AND PAYING therefor during the said term the yearly rent of

TWO THOUSAND ONE HUNDRED AND EIGHTY POUNDS (£2180) clear of

all deductions (except as hereinafter mentioned) by equal

quarterly payments on the usual quarter days in every year

the first of such payments to be made on the 10th day of

April next

2   THE Lessee hereby covenants with the Lessor as

follows

8.9 **A FORM**

Figure 8.8 illustrates a form that could be produced on a word processor with a good quality dot matrix or laser printer. This form could then be recalled and variable text entered as required.

WHAT TO CONSIDER:

1.   How to do *line* and *box draw*.

2.   Can your printer reproduce *straight lines* perfectly?

3.   How to *recall* a standard document (mask) into a new document.

4.   Use *typeover mode* for entering text into the boxes.

5.   Use *stop codes* to move to the places for variable information.

Fig 8.8 *Processing a form*

```
APPLICATION FORM    P765        Married/Single

Name:                           Children:_____
Address:
                                Male/Female

                                Nationality
Telephone (home):               _____
         (work):                Age      _____
                                Car Owner Y/N

EDUCATIONAL QUALIFICATIONS:




EMPLOYMENT DETAILS:



SKILLS:

INTERESTS:

POSITIONS OF RESPONSIBILITY:

For Office Use        Appearance:      Attitude:

Second Interview Y/N
```

THE EIGHT MOST
POPULAR PROGRAMS

9.1 LOCOSCRIPT

(a) Signposts

Locoscript is supplied packaged with all Amstrad PCW 8256, 8512 and 9512 computers (see Glossary). It is supplied on side 2 of the disk that contains the CP/M PLUS (see Glossary) operating system. This is the only word processing program described in this book that does not use MS-DOS. Luckily, as far as you are concerned, there is little discernable difference between the two. The first thing to do is to make a copy of both sides of the disk as supplied to you, using the **DISKIT** program. CP/M is on one side of the disk supplied and Locoscript is on the other. Copy each side onto one side of a new disk. The manual supplied with the machine tells you how to do this.

(b) Basic

The first point to notice about the way that this program works on the PCW series of computers is that in addition to the storage on the single disk (PCW8256 drive **A**) or on the two disks (PCW8512 drive **A** and **B**) there is additional storage available on a "phantom" drive called drive **M**. This is an area of RAM (the internal memory) that acts like a very fast disk drive. It works in exactly the same way as a floppy disk with the important exception that when the computer is switched off *everything stored in it is lost*. It must therefore be treated with care and anything stored on it during a work session must eventually be transferred to disk if you want to keep a permanent record of your work. Locoscript arranges for each disk to be divided into a series of "groups". These are sections of the disk that act like drawers of a filing cabinet so that you can keep documents that have certain features in common together and separate from other sets of documents. The contents of each group are displayed in one of the boxes at the bottom of the screen. These groups are displayed on the screen when Locoscript is started.

Once you have loaded Locoscript it is very simple to create a new document, edit an existing document and print a document. No complicated printer instructions are required because the word processor is supplied as a complete package with computer, programs and printer all ready for use.

(c) Advanced

As supplied with the PCW series of computers Locoscript has few extra-special features. You can *combine* documents together, change the *typeface* and move text about. The most useful "extra" is the ability to store *phrases* and short sections of text for insertion into a document. A maximum of twenty-six phrases can be stored and identified by the letters of the alphabet. A phrase to be stored is marked as a block and then saved away. It is recalled whenever needed by pressing the **PASTE** key followed by its identifying letter. The phrase file can contain up to 550 characters and no phrase can exceed 255 characters in length.

A number of very useful *utilities* come with Locoscript. The commands are issued from the opening menu screen and use the function keys. Documents can be copied from one group into another (**F3**), moved between groups (**F4**), erased (**F6**) and renamed (**F5**). Locoscript has a facility for converting files from its own format into ASCII files that can be read by a number of other computer programs (**F7**).

A *mail-merge* program (called Locomail) and a *spelling checker* (called Locospell) (see Glossary) are available as additional programs to run in conjunction with Locoscript.

(d) How it works

All Locoscript commands are carried out by selecting from a "pull down" menu. These are selected by using one of the four function keys, each of which controls two commands.

Start up

Locoscript is started by first of all placing the program disk into drive **A** with the Locoscript program facing to the left. Switch the computer on and Locoscript loads automatically.

The opening menu lists all the *commands available* at that point; one of these allows you to create a new document or edit an old document.

Create Document

A document is *selected for editing* by moving the cursor through the file directory on the top section of the screen. Each group can be associated with a particular "template" which is a definition of the layout of each document in that group detailing its page width, tab stops and other standard features.

A *ruler line* displayed at the top of the screen shows you the positions of the left and right margins and the tab stops. The status of your document is shown in the first three lines of the display. The first line tells you the name of the document and its group together with the state of the word processor (editing text at this point) and the disk drive currently in use. On the second line you are told the pitch of the printed document and the line spacing. Eight functions are available on the four function keys. These allow you to change the typeface and the pitch, for example, within your document. Each function key has two functions, one when pressed on its own and another when pressed in conjunction with the **Shift** key.

You should notice that by default all the control characters are displayed on the screen embedded in the text, but these can be switched off in order to leave you with a clean screen. Press the **EXIT** key you to leave the document, save it and print it if you wish. The **EXIT** key, by the way, acts as the **Esc** key there being no key of this name on the PCW keyboard.

The PCW range of word processors have a number of pre-programmed keys for use with Locoscript. You can move around text by using the **EOL** (End Of Line), **WORD**, **LINE**, **PARA**, **DOC** and **PAGE** keys.

Insert and Delete

Locoscript enables you to delete anything from one character to a whole block of text. The **Del** **<---** key deletes characters to the *left* and the **Del** **--->** deletes characters to the *right*. Use the **CUT** key together with the **WORD**, **PAGE**, **LINE** and **PARA** keys to mark and delete larger portions of text.

Pages

As you enter text into your document Loco-script displays a solid line under the text that moves down as you add extra lines. When you start a new page this line remains static and a new end-of-page line appears. To force a new page, you choose the "**end page here**" option from the Pages menu or press the **Alt** and **Return** keys at the same time. From this menu also you can arrange to keep a fixed number of lines together at the bottom of a page to avoid widows and orphans.

Saving and Printing

You can either *print* a document as you save it, as described in the previous paragraph, or you can *select* a document from the opening menu and press **P** followed by the **Enter** key. Printer instructions can be entered by pressing the **PTR** key when a new set of options appears at the top of the screen.

Locoscript offers you the facility of "direct printing" which allows you to use the system in *typewriter mode*. Press **D** when the opening menu is displayed and you are presented with an empty screen onto which you can type lines of text. When you press the **Return** key the text is printed directly. This enables you to create and edit text on the screen and print it immediately once you are sure that it has no errors. This is useful for the creation of single "one-off" letters and memos that you have no need to store away on disk.

Cut and Paste

You can insert whole documents in your current document by using the **F7** (Modes) key. As with all these function keys a menu "pulls down" from the top of the screen giving you the options available. When you have made your choice you are then returned tc the opening menu where all the saved files are displayed. You then choose the text to be entered. The text having been chosen it is inserted and you can return to your editing.

Sections of text can be moved about by using the keys marked **COPY** and **PASTE** in conjunction with the **CUT** key.

The *menus* available while you are using Locoscript are

Menu	Settings
Show	Codes
	Rulers
	Blanks
	Spaces
	Effectors
Layout	Insert layout
	Edit layout
Emphasis	Underline
	Bold
	Double
	Reverse Video
Style	Italic
	Half height
	Pitch
Lines	Centre line
	Right justify line
	Insert soft space
	Insert hard space
	Insert soft hyphen
	Insert hard hyphen
	Line spacing
	Line pitch
Pages	Last line of page
	End page here
	Keep lines together
	Insert page number
Modes	Disc management
	Edit Identify text
	Edit header
	Insert text
Blocks	Block
	Save block
	Phrase
	Save all phrases

9.2 WORDSTAR^{1512}

(a) Signposts

The first thing you will discover when you use the WordStar^{1512} (see Glossary) word processor is that it bears no relationship to the WordStar word processor described below in Section 9.5. Their only point in common is that they can read each other's files without any conversion being necessary. This program was designed to be used on the Amstrad PC1512 computer, although it can be run quite easily on any PC with one or two floppy disk drives or a hard disk and a single floppy disk drive. WordStar^{1512} is supplied on six floppy disks together with a manual and your first task is to instal the program so as to run on your particular computer system. Details of how this is to be done are given in the manual. The actual installation is very simple, but takes a little time. Part of the installation involves telling the program what printer you are using. You can choose any three printers from over two hundred that WordStar^{1512} can use. Even if you have one printer only you can arrange for the program to print in *draft mode*, which is fast but not very high quality, or *NLQ* which is slower but much better. Or you can choose between feeding continuous stationery and single sheets. Each of these modes are treated as a *different printer* by WordStar^{1512}.

(b) Basic

Wordstar^{1512} is totally *menu-driven* so that at every stage in the creation, editing and printing of a document - together with the other features offered by this program - you select your requirement from a menu that pulls down from the top of the screen. Your choice is made by moving a highlight to the required function and pressing the **Return** key to put it into action.

Text can easily be edited by using the **Delete** and **Insert** keys on the keyboard. You can leave any part of the word processor at any time by pressing the **Escape** key. This makes it particularly easy for you to get out of any trouble you might have caused by accident.

(c) Advanced

WordStar[1512] provides a number of special features. One of these is a *simple mail-merge* facility that is based upon a series of "*file cards*" called a Master List. This feature allows you to complete a ready-designed "form" on the screen containing such data as surname, first names, address, company name and telephone number. A selection procedure allows you to pick all those entries with certain pieces of data in common for inclusion in a mailing list. You can use this feature in conjunction with a standard letter into which details from selected "file cards" can be inserted so that a letter can be sent, say, to all the vets that live in Buckinghamshire.
A *spelling checker* is provided while you are editing or creating a document. By means of this the whole document can be spell-checked and alternatives offered when an unrecognisable word is found.
Label printing can be performed very simply in Word-Star[1512] since a set of pre-programmed formats are available so that you can print labels of any size and layout with ease. The names and addresses to be printed on the labels are again taken from the "file cards" on the appropriate master list.

(d) How it works

WordStar[1512] is easy to use if you follow the menus that are displayed on the screen at every point. There is copious **Help** available by pressing the **F1** key. If you are using a machine with floppy disk drives only then you will find that the program is slow to operate and you spend a considerable amount of time changing the disk in drive **A**. There are five to choose from. On a hard disk system this problem does not exist.

Start up

If your computer has floppy disk drives then you must start up WordStar[1512] by placing the disk called "**WordStar[1512] System**" in the main drive and typing

ws1512

at the operating system **A>** prompt. If you have
a hard disk system you will already have the
program on the hard disk and so all you need
to do is to type the

ws1512

at the **C>**. Choose the **Word Processing** option
from the opening menu and follow the instructions that appear on the screen.

If you choose the **File Management** option from
the opening menu you will be presented with a
further menu that enables you to choose any
one of four file operations. These enable you
to delete, rename, copy or move files between
disks or sub-directories of a hard disk.
Copying is an essential operation particularly
if you are operating on one disk drive only.
You have to store all your documents in the
RAM disk and copy them onto a floppy disk for
safety once you have completed your work. In
addition you should always have at least *two*
copies of every document, kept in separate
places, in case of accidents. Once you have
mastered the discipline of looking at the
instructions given to you on the menus you
will find that WordStar^{1512} is a very easy and
powerful word processor to use.

Create Document

If you have a single drive computer then you
create all your documents in the RAM drive and
copy them onto disk at the end of the session.
If you have a twin disk machine the document
disk goes in drive **B**. All documents are
automatically stored on the hard disk if you
have that type of machine.

WordStar^{1512} *remembers the last document* you
edited and so you will have to overtype its
name in the highlighted box on the screen with
the name of your new document. Having completed that the screen will change to a blank

document screen with a ruler line and status line. You should note that the top right-hand corner of every WordStar^{1512} screen contains a list of the commands you can issue at that point. You will always see the injunction to press **Esc** if you want to get out from that screen and that you press the **F1** key for help. The **F2** key, also noted at the top right of the screen, gives you access to the *editing menus*. These menus allow you to set tabs and margins, centre text, find and replace text and set the style of the final document.

Select the feature from the menu to turn it on and then select it again when you wish to turn it off.

Once you have entered your document you leave the menu by pressing the **Esc** key and this gives you the option of abandoning the document or saving it. You then return to the main word processing menu from which you can create or edit another document or print a document by pressing **Esc** again which will bring you back to the opening menu.

Cursor movement is by means of the arrow keys. On their own these keys move you up or down by one line and left or right by one character. A left or right arrow key in conjunction with the **Ctrl** key moves you one word left or right. **Ctrl** and the **Home** or **End** key takes you to the beginning or end of the current line. The **PgUp** and **PgDn** keys take you forwards or backwards by one screenful, whereas these keys in conjunction with the **Ctrl** key take you to the beginning or end of the document. To delete a line of your text press **Ctrl** and **Backspace**. A deleted line can be restored as mentioned earlier. A blank line is created by pressing the **Ctrl** key and the **Return** key simultaneously.

Insert

The **Ins** key controls the toggle that allows insertion of characters into the current text.

If you are in Insert Mode then you are informed by a message at the top of the ruler line. A blank line is inserted by pressing **Ctrl** and **Return**.

Delete

The **Backspace** key deletes characters to the left of the cursor and the **Del** key deletes the character under the cursor. Large sections of text are deleting by choosing the **Delete text** option from the editing menu. You mark it and then delete it. Deleted text can be restored to the document.

Pages

A new page is forced by selecting the **End Page** option from the editing menu. The layout of the pages of your document are chosen from the **Change Settings** menu. The **Word Processing** option allows you to amend such things as the numbering of pages and justification and the **Page Layout** option provides you with the chance to alter the page length, size of margins and line length.

Save

When you wish to leave a document press the **Esc** key and the options to quit the document or save it are given.

Print

A document is chosen for printing from the printing menu where you are given the choice of printing the current document (i.e. the one last edited), choosing a document to print, change the print options or choosing one of the three available printers for your output.
By using the **Modify print options** choice from this menu you can select how many copies of your document to print, number the pages and

set the size of the left-hand margin - this provides a **binding width**. If you need to change the layout of the pages of your document then you must return to the opening menu and select the **Change settings** option. This allows you to set the page length, margin sizes to the left and right and at the top and bottom.

Cut and Paste

Text can be moved about within a document by choosing the **Move text** option from the editing menu. The text to moved is marked and then the cursor is taken to its new place in the document. Press **Return** to set the command into operation.

9.3 WORDPERFECT 4.2

(a) Signposts

WordPerfect (see Glossary) is distributed in the UK by Sentinel Software. At the time of going to press (January 1988) 4.2 is the most recent version of this sophisticated program and is therefore the one studied in this section.

(b) Basic

WordPerfect 4.2 has many commands to offer but its major feature must be its *simplicity for the new user*. There are no confusing initial menus, just what appears to represent a blank sheet of paper. This gives the new user great confidence.

As soon as you start up WordPerfect you are faced with a blank workscreen. This is where you can create a new document, then name it and save it. Alternatively you can clear the workscreen without saving the document at all. You can *retrieve* a previously created document into the blank workscreen. If you already have a document on the screen then this same **retrieve** command may be used to *combine* documents.

When you want to *print a file* you can retrieve it to

the workscreen and print it, either page by page or all at once. Alternatively you can print one file while working on another.

(c) Advanced

Those people who need to use sophisticated features will find WordPerfect invaluable. Perhaps one of its biggest assets is the way you can form a *print queue* for a number of documents, selecting pages and printers for them, while working on two other documents concurrently. Because a large portion of WordPerfect can be put into memory you can take the disks out and call in documents from other disks while a document is displayed on the screen. You can even remove a disk that contains the file that is being printed without risk.

With a laser printer a great number of *fonts* can be used. With a good quality dot matrix printer using pitch **13*** and font **3** the printout is good enough to be camera-ready. That is what we used for this book. There is a **macro** feature, which can save both commands and text of any size.

Page numbering has never been so simple or versatile and you don't need to use headers and footers to accomplish this. The **headers and footers** feature works for all pages or alternate pages which is a boon to in-house publishers.

The addition of the **"switch" screens** command means that you can switch from one document to another without having to save one first. Use this for reference purposes or to copy text between documents. The **window** feature means that two documents may be displayed one above the other to be used with the switch command.

The **maths** features can not only perform simple calculations on blocks of text but also offers a **mini-spread-sheet** facility.

Merge is simple to use and merge records can have differing numbers of lines while variable information can include carriage returns. If you make one mistake in an early record this will not affect subsequent pages. **Sort** allows you to sort by line, field or record in a merge and is straightforward to use.

Parallel or **Newspaper** columns are simple to generate and use.

Authors will be thrilled with the simplicity of the **index**, **table of contents** and **list** generation features, the only drawback being that files of over 13K are possibly too large for the index to cope with if you are using a dual floppy drive machine.

There is a **spelling checker** facility which works extremely fast and offers sensible alternatives for unrecognised words. If the correct spelling is still not found then you can try a **phonetic look-up**. Personal dictionaries may be created and used. You can check the spelling of a word, page or document, even a marked block, after which a **word count** is displayed. However a word count can be carried out without the spelling check.

A **Thesaurus** facility is supplied which allows you to look up *synonyms* and *antonyms* and then further alternatives for the words offered.

(d) How it works

All WordPerfect commands are carried out by means of *function keys*, around which a **help** template fits, on your keyboard. Press a key on its own or at the same time as the **Alt**, **Control** or **Shift** key. In this way there are 40 commands at your fingertips.

The **Control** key is also used with the **arrow keys**, **delete**, **backspace** and **Enter** to access more commands still.

When you issue a command from the function keys you will often see a menu. The menu will either run along the base of the screen or will replace the text on your screen until you have made your selection. You will find that each menu option will be given either a number or a letter. Press that number or letter to select the option you require. If you want to clear a menu from your screen without using it the **Cancel** key will usually do this for you.

The **Cancel** key **(F1)** is usually your "Get out of trouble" command. The **Exit (F7)** key is usually your "Yes please and go back to the workscreen" command. In WordPerfect the **Esc** key is used to *repeat keystrokes*.

Each time that you issue a command that changes the

format of your document (such as **Tab** or **Page Break**) you change the margins or alter the page length, a **code** will be embedded in the text. This code reminds you when you gave the command. All subsequent text will adhere to the command represented by the code. If you delete a code you also delete its effect. Although codes are not visible while you are working they can be *revealed* at any time. When they are revealed the codes are enclosed in square brackets, e.g. **[TAB]**, and may be deleted with the **Del** or **Backspace** keys.

Start up

When the **A>** or **C>** is displayed, key-in **wp** and press **Enter** to load WordPerfect into memory. If you want to access the **Set-up** menu and alter any defaults key-in **wp/s**. If you want to load more WordPerfect into memory in order to make it work faster key-in **wp/r**.

Create Document

As soon as WordPerfect is loaded into memory the blank workscreen is displayed with the **status line** in the lower right hand corner. Key-in your document from here, default upper, lower, left and right margins are suitable for A4 paper using a one inch letterhead.

Text will automatically insert to the left of the cursor. The **Ins** key is used to toggle between **Insert** and **Typeover** modes. Use the arrow keys for cursor movement. Use the **Home** key followed by either one or two arrow keys to move quickly about the document.

You do not need to name a document until you *save* it.

Delete

You can delete single characters or single words, from the cursor to the end of the line or the end of the page. If you mark text as a block the block may then be deleted by pressing **Del**. The **Cancel** command will restore the last text deleted.

Pages

A *system page break* will appear after 54
lines, unless the default has been changed. It
looks like a row of hyphens. Enter a manual
page break with **Ctrl Enter**. It appears on the
screen as a double row of hyphens.

You can alter the page length as often as you
like and even ask for pages to be *centred* from
top to bottom.

Print

You can print the document on the screen by
block, page or in its entirety. The **Print
Options** allow you to switch from hand-fed to
sheet-fed stationery and from printer to
printer while the document is on the screen.

You can switch to the **List Files** screen and
print any number of documents from there.
Alternatively you can print named documents
with selected pages from within another
document.

Save

A document must be *displayed on the screen*
before it may be saved. When it is saved you
can return to it immediately, clear the workscreen or exit WordPerfect. It is simple to
rename and save a file.

Cut and Paste

You can cut and paste sentences, paragraphs or
words. Alternatively you can mark a piece of
text as a block and then move, copy, save or
delete it.

You are also able to cut and paste *rectangles*
and *columns*.

9.4 MULTIMATE ADVANTAGE II

(a) Signposts

MultiMate Advantage II (see Glossary) is the improved version of MultiMate Advantage and came onto the market in 1987. MultiMate Advantage itself was the updated version of MultiMate. Most commands have not altered so users who are migrating from one version to another will have no problems finding their way around.

MultiMate Advantage II is straightforward to use as a word processor and is supplied with **On-file**, an additional program used for managing information in a database.

(b) Basic

The new user will find MultiMate Advantage II remarkably easy to use. Pull-down menus have been incorporated into the original program as an option. In this way you can still use the original commands if you prefer. However, if you are unsure of a command you can press **Alt L**. This displays the menus from which you can select the required feature. As you highlight each menu option an *explanation of that feature* is displayed at the base of the screen.

The **Help (Shift F1)** is good but hardly necessary owing to the help that is included when pull-down menus are used.

The commands are consistent so it is easy to move around the menus and screens without trouble.

When you start word processing its main menu is displayed and the wording is clear. As you create a new document the file directory is displayed. You are also shown how much space remains on the logged disk.

A document may be printed without saving it first which is useful for *draft copies*; there is also a draft print facility which is faster than normal print because it uses less ink from the ribbon.

(c) Advanced

You are now able to make MultiMate Advantage II work more efficiently than its predecessor. Even on a dual floppy system the functions work faster than ever before. The pull-down menus make it easy to use new features while the most basic commands can be carried out with the minimum keystrokes.

If you are already familiar with another word processor you could use MultiMate Advantage II without looking at the manual! Menus are full of explanations and help. Complicated functions are easy to follow.

It is easy to change defaults for drives, documents and the system so it is not necessary to reinstal the system disk every time you change printer. During initial installation you will have to select the printer table (**PAT**), sheet feeder table (**SAT**) and character translation width table (**CWT**) files that are to be copied from the disks provided onto the system disk. Once this has been completed selection is straightforward and can be carried out from the print parameters menu.

This new version of MultiMate no longer starts each new page at the top of the screen. Instead the format line is used to separate pages and the cursor can scroll through the document quickly.

There are 9 **pitches** available producing from 5.0 to 17.6 characters per inch. Pitch can be changed from within a document as often as required.

Headers and **footers** are simple to create, cancel and use. The system date and/or time can be included together with the document name, system page number and last page number of the document. There are both **footnote** and **endnote** facilities too.

Maths calculations can be carried out for vertical or horizontal columns.

Sort is simple to use and if you use the **information handling** facility you can create a mini database (using a template you create yourself) that can be used for **merge** and **sort**. A standard **merge** is very easy to create and use but also time consuming as there is a lot of repetition. Unless you set up a key procedure (macro) which produces the symbols in the data file for you it can be a lengthy process. Use the **information handling** facility when you want to work only with a maximum of 255 records. Use the **On-file** utility when you want to work with vast amount of information.

Parallel or **newspaper** columns are simple to generate and use.

A **table of contents** can be generated from a document by creating a **.TOC** file while working on the main file which can then be generated and printed.

Line and box draw uses six different characters which can be used for drawing lines.

Documents may be **spell checked** (which flags unrecognised words), and then **spell edited** which offers alternatives for the unrecognised words. New words may then be added to your choice of **custom dictionary**.

The **Thesaurus** facility will offer alternatives and definitions for words or phrases.

If you want to save a short phrase or set of commands you can use the **key procedure** command. For longer sections of text you can create a **library** which is then attached to your document and from which selected sections can be retrieved.

The **section numbering** feature is invaluable if you write long reports.

Although messages are displayed to help with **cut and paste** operations this is the program's *weakest feature*. You can copy text from one file into the current file but not vice versa. Unfortunately there is no quick way to call all of one document into the current document.

(d) How it works

MultiMate Advantage II is supplied with detailed manuals, a teaching disk and a set of stickers that can be attached to the function keys on the keyboard. These stickers will remind you of the commands controlled by the keys. The **Shift**, **Control** and **Alt** keys may be depressed with the function keys to access further commands while the **Alt** key may be used with the letter keys for more commands still. Use **Control** with the keys on the numeric pad to access the commands that move the cursor around the document quickly.

If you are unsure of a function press **Alt L** which activates the pull-down menus. Use the **up and down arrow keys** to move the block cursor through the menu. This displays information about the feature. Press **F10** to use the highlighted feature or **Esc** to remove the menus from the screen. Use the left and right arrow keys to access additional menus from the one currently displayed.

The **Esc** key is usually your "Get out of trouble key".

The **F10** key is usually your "Yes please and continue" key.

Whenever you press a key such as **Tab** or **Indent**, a symbol will be displayed on the screen at the cursor position. If you delete the symbol you also delete its effect.

Start up

MultiMate Advantage II is supplied with its own boot disk. Use this to boot up to the **A>** if you are using a dual floppy machine. If you have a machine with a hard disk, boot up will be automatic. See Section 1.4 for a full explanation of the boot up procedure.

When the **A>** or **C>** is displayed key-in **wp** and press **Enter** to load MultiMate Advantage II into memory. This displays the main menu. Notice how the **Word Processing** option is number **1** in the menu. Key-in **1**.

If you have a dual floppy machine you will be asked to exchange the boot disk in drive **A** for the system disk and strike a key to continue.

The word processing main menu is now displayed.

If you *want to go straight into word processing* without using the MultiMate Advantage main menu key-in **mm** from the **A>** or **C>**. If you are using a dual floppy machine you will have to exchange the boot disk or the system disk first.

Create Document

As soon as you have entered word processing the main menu is displayed. Each option has been given a number. Key-in that number followed by **Enter** to select an option.

Key-in **2** and then press **Enter** which displays the **Create New Document** screen.

Key-in a new name for your document and alter the drive/directory specification if necessary. Press **F10** when you have finished to display the **Document Summary** screen.

Key-in any information you want at this point. Press **F10** when you have finished to display the **Modify Document Defaults** screen which handles the *page layout*.

Move the arrow keys to the responses in this table and overtype any defaults that you wish to change. Press **F10** when you have finished to display the workscreen.

The format line runs along the top of the workscreen. The >> symbol denote each tab-stop and the << symbol denotes the right margin. The number at the left-hand side of the format line denotes the spacing.

Text will overtype unless you press **Ins** to alter the default.

Insert

There are two options available. **Drop down** will move all text after the cursor to the end of the screen so all new text appears in a blank space. **Push** will insert new text to the left of the cursor.

You can insert *single spaces* using the **plus key** on the numeric pad. To insert text, press **Ins**, key-in the new text and press **Ins** once more.

Delete

You can choose whether backspace is to be *destructive* or not from the **System and Document Defaults** option from the word processing menu.

You can *delete* characters one at a time using the **minus key** on the numeric pad. If you want to delete larger chunks of text you can press **Del**, highlight the text to delete and then press **Del** once more.

Pages

You can select whether a *system page break* is inserted or not and after how many lines. The format line is used to separate pages within a document. Use the **page combine** command to delete the page break or press **page** to create a page break.

If your pages are of different lengths you are able to **repaginate** the document according to the ideal number of lines you require per page.

Print

You can print the document on the screen page by page without saving it first. Alternatively you can use the print option from the word processing menu to print named documents and form a *queue*. This option gives you many print parameters which can be changed for each document if required and remain the default until changed once more.

Save

You can save a document without removing it from your screen, save it and return to the word processing menu or save it and go straight to any of the functions listed in the word processing menu.

Cut and Paste

You can cut and paste any amount of text within a document. These commands display messages which remind you which stage you have reached. For example, if you press **COPY (F8)** the **COPY WHAT?** message is displayed. Highlight the text you want to copy and press **F10** to display the **TO WHERE?** message, and so on.

An **external copy** allows you to copy text from *another document* into the current document.

9.5 WORDSTAR 4.0

(a) Signposts

WordStar (see Glossary) in its various forms currently has over 3 million users. Version 4.0 Professional uses the same commands that version 1.0 started out with. Now there are additional commands and more sophisticated functions. However, if you used the earliest of versions you will still have no difficulty using the latest.

WordStar was so named because it was first released before PCs were born; there were few function keys, if any, and no cursor movement keys on the numeric pad. As a result the keys **S**, **D**, **E** and **X** were used to take the cursor to the left, right, up and down respectively. This formed a star shape. To make the cursor work the **Control** key had to be pressed at the same time as the appropriate letter key.

(b) Basic

WordStar is a menu-based program. This makes it easy for the new user as the options available are displayed at the top of the screen. The initial defaults for the layout of a document is such that text will be justified and a page number will print at the base of each page. This can cause frustration in the new user, who will continually forget to remove justification and page numbering before starting to type. However, once this has been mastered WordStar is uncomplicated and straightforward. Version 4 (and indeed version 3.4) have programmed the function keys on the PC keyboard to reproduce some of the most common WordStar commands. This makes life a lot easier.

Although other programs have now learned to "sing and dance", WordStar still chooses to concentrate on the features that are used most often. It offers more **Help** and explanation than some other programs. Without **Help** and the function key translations some of the WordStar commands seem to be arbitrary. For example **Control KD** means **Save** while **Control KY** means **Delete Marked Block**. However, because WordStar does not try to offer features that are of little use to most people, the commands there are can be learned without too much difficulty.

This program has stood the test of time and will always have faithful followers.

When alterations are made to the margins text does not automatically reform to fit between these new margins. Instead the **reform** command must be used for each paragraph. This can be frustrating.

(c) Advanced

WordStar 4.0 provides a **spelling checker** with **personal dictionary** options. You can check the spelling of as much as a whole document or as little as one word. There is a **Thesaurus** feature (called **Wordfinder**) and many other features that earlier versions did not include. There is now little difference between WordStar and its rivals.

Index and **Table of Contents** generation are available and can be created in two different ways. **Dot commands** may be used instead of many **control** commands which can make life easier.

There is a **macro** feature (called **shorthand**) which can reproduce both commands and text. This is easy to used and as the macro names are displayed on the screen it is easy to remember them.

Maths is available and a **calculator** for simple arithmetic and equations.

Merge is easy to use, but there is room for error and data and primary files must be checked with care. However, files created by a database program can often be converted into WordStar format with little effort.

You can have up to three **headers** and three **footers** in a document, these can include the system page number or a different one as required.

A line and box draw feature is available which will produce lines, perfect corners and junctions.

(d) How it works

When you do not have a document on your screen the opening menu lists the available commands and indicates which letter you should press in order to use a feature. When you do have a document on your screen the Editing Menu lists the available commands and indicates which letter you should press **at the same time as** the **Control** key in order to use a feature. The **Control** key is represented by the circumflex symbol . Not all the commands can be displayed on the screen at once so additional menus may be accessed. **Ctrl O** accesses the **Onscreen** menu, **Ctrl J** accesses the **Help** menu, **Ctrl K** accesses the **Block and Save** menu, **Ctrl P** accesses the **Print** menu and **Ctrl Q** accesses the **Quick** menu. As soon as one of these menus is displayed the options available are shown together with the character that should now be pressed in order to use that feature.

The function keys have been programmed to replace some of these commands. The ten keys will perform ten of the WordStar commands; if you press **Shift** with one of these keys ten further commands can be used.

Use the **arrow keys** to move the cursor around the document. If the arrow keys, **home** or **end** are used with **Control** then more efficient cursor movement can be achieved.

The **Ctrl U** command is your "Get out of Trouble Key", sometimes it will need to be followed by **Esc**. The **Return** key is your "Yes" key.

Start up

When the **A>** or **C>** is displayed key-in **ws** and press **Enter** to load WordStar into memory.

Create Document

Display the opening menu at the top of the screen with the current file directory beneath it.

Key-in **d** to display instructions about the naming of files. When you have named your file press **Enter** to display the **File Does Not Exist. Create a New One? Y** message. Press **y** and the blank workscreen will be displayed.

The editing menu is displayed at the top of the screen. All text will wrap round the screen. The system defaults to justify text between margins. The ruler line runs along the base of the editing menu and indicates left and right margins, tabs with **!** symbols and decimal tabs with **#** symbols. The status line runs along the top of the editing menu and shows the position of the cursor.

Insert

The system defaults to insert all text to the left of the cursor. If you want to overtype text press **Ins**, this is a toggle.

Delete

You can delete text one character at a time, one word at a time, one line at a time or from the cursor to the right side or left side of the line. You can also delete a marked block in one go. The **undo** command will restore the last text deleted.

Pages

The system defaults to produce a page break after every 54 lines. This appears as a row of hyphens across the screen. To set your own page break key-in **.pa** with the **.** in the first column of the appropriate line. You can alter the length of the page, the size of the upper and lower margins and the length of the text at any time.

Print

A document must be *saved before it is printed*. It is usual to save the document then select **P** for print from the opening menu and answer the print parameters one at a time. If all the default options are appropriate you can press **Esc** to ignore them.

  To save the current document and go straight to the print parameters press **Control Prt Sc**.

Cut and Paste

You can move and copy any amount of text within one document. You can also copy a

marked block of text from the current document
out into a completely new document and copy a
different document into the current one.

9.6 WORDSTAR 2000

(a) Signposts

WordStar 2000 was also developed by MicroPro Inc. It was
designed to take the legwork out of traditional WordStar
and make it easier to use. Commands became more logical
while the structure of the program remained the same.

(b) Basic

A new user will find the commands are straightforward,
in fact many of them can be guessed at. The Opening Menu
appears once WordStar 2000 has been loaded into memory
and will guide you around the available options. A
number of pre-set formats are provided to help you set
out your documents according to your requirements and
thus minimise the amount of tab, margins and justification adjustments. A *format has to be selected* for your
document before it can be created. A format can be
altered at any point in order that it may suit your
needs more fully. There is **MEMO.FRM** that sets the layout
for a memorandum automatically, **JUSTIFY.FRM** that
produces justified text and **RAGGED.FRM** that produces
text with a ragged right-hand margin, and so on.
  There is plenty of **help** and instruction on the screen
so the new user should have no trouble learning WordStar
2000.
  If you want to use WordStar 2000 as a typewriter for
letters, envelopes or filling in forms then **typewriter
mode** is invaluable.

(c) Advanced

There are many sophisticated features supplied with
WordStar 2000, the **window** feature being among the most
useful. This allows you to copy and move text between
documents simply and efficiently. It also allows you to
refer to one document - or part of the current document
- while working on a different document or at a dif-

ferent position in the same document.

You can tailormake your own document layouts, called **formats**, which can then be attached to your documents and save time.

There is a **macro** facility called **key glossary** which will help you to save and recall text and commands as quickly as possible.

The **maths** feature allows you to perform calculations on marked blocks of text.

The **sort** feature will sort marked blocks of text into alphabetical order,ascending or descending.

Files can be **converted** from normal WordStar into WordStar 2000 simply and quickly.

Merge is very easy to use indeed as the commands are well explained and follow a definite pattern.

(d) How it works

When you do not have a document on your screen, the opening menu lists the available commands and indicates which letter you should press in order to use a feature. When you do have a document on your screen, the editing menu lists the available commands and indicates which letter you should press **at the same time as** the **Control** key in order to use a feature. The **Control** key is represented on the screen by the circumflex symbol . Not all the commands can be displayed on the screen at once so additional menus may be accessed. **Ctrl O** accesses the **Options** menu, **Ctrl G** accesses the **Get Help** menu, **Ctrl B** accesses the **Block** menu, **Ctrl P** accesses the **Print Enhancement** menu, **Ctrl T** accesses the **Tabs and Margins** menu, **Ctrl R** accesses the **Remove** menu, **Ctrl L** accesses the **Locate** menu, **Ctrl C** accesses the **Cursor** menu, **Ctrl K** accesses the **Key Glossary** menu and **Ctrl Q** accesses the **Quit** menu. As soon as one of these menus is displayed the options available are shown together with the character that should now be pressed in order to use that feature. For example **Ctrl CB** is the command that will take the **C**ursor to the **B**eginning of the file, so you would press **Ctrl** C to display the **cursor** menu, which would show you to press **B** to take the cursor to the beginning of the file.

Use the **arrow keys** to move the cursor about the document. Combine the keys on the numeric pad with the

Control key to achieve more efficient cursor movement.
The **Ctrl U** command is your "Get out of Trouble Key",
sometimes it will need to be followed by **Esc**. The **Return**
key is your "Yes" key.

Start up

When the **A>** or **C>** is displayed key-in **ws2** and
press **Enter** to load WordStar 2000 into memory.

Create Document

Display the opening menu at the top of the
screen. You will see that there is a second
opening menu. Press **spacebar** to see this.
Key-in **e** to display instructions about the
naming of files. When you have named your file
press **Enter** to display information about
attaching a format to your document.
A list of formats is displayed with the **block
cursor** on the first of these. Press the **arrow
keys** to move the block cursor about the list.
When you have highlighted the format you
require press **Enter** and the workscreen will be
displayed.
Text will automatically insert to the left of
the cursor and wrap round the screen as you
type. The editing menu is displayed at the top
of the screen and shows the available options.
The status line runs along the top of the
editing menu and gives information about the
cursor position. The ruler lines gives the
position of the tabs and margins and runs
along the base of the editing menu. Each
triangle represents a *tab stop*, each vertical
line represents a *margin*.

Insert

The system defaults to insert all text to the
left of the cursor. If you want to overtype
text press **Ins**, this is a toggle.

Delete

You can delete text one character at a time, one word at a time, one line at a time or from the cursor to the right side or left side of the line. You can also delete a marked block in one go.

Pages

The system defaults to produce a *page break* after every 54 lines, or according to the default set in the document format. This appears as a row of hyphens across the screen. To set your own page break press **Ctrl OP** at the start of the appropriate line. You can alter the length of the page, the size of the upper and lower margins and the length of the text at any time.

Print

A document must be *saved before it is printed*. It is usual to save the document then select **P** for print from the opening menu and answer the print parameters one at a time. If all the default options are appropriate you can press **Ctrl Q** to ignore them.

Cut and Paste

You can move and copy any amount of text within one document. You can also copy a marked block of text from the current document out into a completely new document and copy a different document into the current one. Owing to the **window facility** you can also copy and move marked blocks of text of any size from one document to another.

9.7   DISPLAYWRITE 4

(a) Signposts

The DisplayWrite programs (see Glossary) were designed to replace the IBM Displaywriter dedicated word processors as PCs became more and more popular. It has become a sophisticated and powerful program, popular with companies who have frequent communications with the United States.

(b) Basic

The new user should love DisplayWrite 4. It is menu-driven and the selection of an option from a menu is foolproof. In main menus each option can be selected by pressing its initial letter, its identifying number or by moving the block cursor to cover that option and pressing **Enter**. Pop-up menus have been introduced to help you find your way around the program though some commands can be used without going through a menu.

The **Help** is very comprehensive indeed and a new user would be wise to read the help screens page by page before starting to use the program.

A keyboard template is provided to remind you which keys are used for which functions and this is very necessary. However, translations of the major function keys run along the top of the workscreen.

Some menus are confusing - they offer too many commands which, though necessary, may worry a new user.

(c) Advanced

There is even a facility for a recorded **voice message** with DisplayWrite 4! This is a sophisticated program and offers many useful features in addition to the most traditional ones. Some of the complicated and less useful features may have been added at the expense of the most frequently-used commands. However, this is a powerful program and advanced features cannot be achieved without the help of the manual.

You can change the **format** for your document as often as you like and text between two format commands will be fixed for that section. The default format can be changed for the whole document and if you have a format that you like to use frequently you can create a **profile** which can then be activated and become the default as required.

You can set a **page break** that will be moved by **repagination** or one that will not be affected during repagination. **Page length** can be set as required for each document or you can change the default.

DisplayWrite 4 offers **headers**, **footers** and **footnotes**. Headers and footers can be set for alternate pages and are simple to start and cancel.

The **spelling checker** allows you to flag all unrecognised words or to offer alternative spellings. **Custom dictionaries** can be created, and attached as required. **Repagination** can be undertaken during a spelling check if required.

The **Housekeeping** facilities allow the use of **wild-cards** which saves a considerable amount of time.

There is a **macro** feature, called **key programming**.

You can **underline** text in three different ways: one word at a time, by using the underline command at the start and end of the text to underline, or by marking the text as a block. If you want to remove both **bold** and **underline** from a block of text, you can do this at the same time, by making it **plain**.

Text for revision can be **marked** so that this is made clear to the operator.

Document **comments** are encouraged, as they may be displayed with the **file directory** which helps you to recognise a filename.

When you issue the command to edit, print, delete, copy or rename a file, for example, you can display the file directory and select the required file at this point.

Although the **merge** program is lengthy to use, there are alternatives. **Stop codes** can be set in a mask document and then this document can be recalled and the cursor taken directly to a stop code so that variable information can be added.

The **include** feature allows you to embed a code in a document that will recall another file at that point. If you ask to include a file that contains an include command itself then you can choose whether to start this chain reaction or not.

There is a **cursor draw** feature which will help you

produce professional forms.

The **table layout** feature will lay out your columns according to the parameters you request. In this way you do not have to set any tabs for the columns.

The **math** feature is fairly sophisticated as it can add, subtract, multiply and divide numbers, use constants or perform calculations on a block.

When margins are altered text will not automatically reform to fit between the new margins. Instead you need to use the **line adjust** command. This can be very time consuming.

A **notepad** is used for the storage of information temporarily. When you need to **cut and paste** you can copy the text out to the notepad and then back again as required.

(d) How it works

When you do not have a document on your screen you should see the opening menu, from which you can make your selections.

When you are editing a document a translation of the most important function keys runs along the top of the screen. Press a function key and a menu will be displayed. In order to make a selection from one of these menus you can press the corresponding number, the first letter of the required feature (or otherwise as indicated) or move the arrow keys to highlight the required option with the block cursor and press **Enter**.

Additional commands are accessed by pressing **Ctrl** with either a function key or a letter key.

While you are carrying out a command there will often be a help message at the base of the screen, such as

MOVE CURSOR TO END OF BLOCK AND PRESS ENTER

during block work.

When ever you press the **Tab** key, **Indent**, or change the format for example, a code will be embedded in the document. The code will be displayed only when the cursor is in that space. Then the explanation of that code will be displayed in the left-hand corner of the status line. If you want to display the codes all the time you need to use the edit options screen (**Ctrl F5**).

You will find that **Esc** is your "Get out of Trouble" key and **Enter** is your "Yes" key.

Start up

As soon as the **A>** or **C>** is displayed key-in **dw4** and press **Enter**. After a few seconds the IBM logo is displayed together with a request to press **Enter** to start DisplayWrite 4. If you have trouble starting up check that the printer is on and ready.

Create Document

When the opening menu is on your screen select the **Create a Document** option (menu selection is explained earlier) to display the **Create Document** screen.

Key-in a name for the document. If you need to look at the file directory press **F3**.

Press the **down-arrow key** if you want to enter a comment. This will be displayed with the file directory and is useful for reference.

When you are ready press **Enter** to display the workscreen.

The status lines run along the two upper lines of the screen and gives information about the current cursor position and the current pitch, keyboard and level of program. The left-hand side is used to display the translation of the embedded codes in your document.

The *scale line* shows the current tab and margin settings. Each number indicates the column (in tens), each tab is indicated by an underline symbol, while the left and right margins are shown by the << and >> symbols. A triangle shows the middle of the screen.

Text wraps round the screen and is displayed unjustified. Text will overtype unless the **Ins** key is pressed.

Use the arrow keys on the numeric pad to move the cursor, when you use the left and right arrow keys with the **Ctrl** key the cursor will move from word to word. The **home** and **end** keys are used to take the cursor from one side of the line to the other. In DisplayWrite 4 the cursor *does not wrap around the screen* as for other programs.

Insert

Use the **Ins** key to *toggle* between insert and overtype modes.

Delete

You can delete text one character at a time or in large chunks by marking it as a block first. The **restore delete** command will restore the last text deleted.

Pages

A new page always starts at the top of the screen if you make a page break. A page break (**Ctrl E**) is soft while a required page break (**Ctrl R**) is hard. Pages can be sorted out only by **repagination** unless you use **Ctrl E** each time and do not make any alterations. Page length may be set through the **page layout** option in the **format** menu.

Print

A document must be *saved before it can be printed*. The last document used will always be the default. If you need to view the file directory press **F3** and select the file name from here.

You can select **background** or **foreground** printing. the former will allow you to form a *queue*.

Save

You can save a file and return to the opening menu, save it and continue working on it, or quit any changes you have made.

Cut and Paste

You can move and copy any amount of text within the same document or between documents. In order to copy text *between* documents you need to copy the text to the **notepad** from the source document, display the target document on the screen and then copy the text in from the notepad.

However, if you want to copy text from one file into the current file you can use the **include** or **get** command which allows you to specify the pages required.

9.8   WORDCRAFT 3

(a) Signposts

Wordcraft (see Glossary) is a word processing program designed to keep up with the needs of the modern office. WordCraft 3 was developed in 1987 and offers sophisticated functions in addition to the utilities: Formaster 2, for designing forms; Imagemaster, for incorporating graphics and scans into a WordCraft document; Toolkit, for converting files from dBASE III, indexing large documents, extra technical information and a DCA file convertor. WordCraft Nova was developed to cater for people who require a low cost program with no fancy utilities or unnecessary commands.

(b) Basic

When WordCraft is loaded the workscreen is displayed. Text can then be recalled or created on this workscreen. At first glance WordCraft is confusing. In order to carry out some commands you need to be in **command mode**, to key-in text you need to be in **type mode** and the **Esc** key is used to **toggle** from one to the other. If you need to produce and print simple letters then WordCraft is very easy to use. For example, you would key-in **print** to print the document on the screen, **save** to save it and **new** to get a new, blank workscreen. However, as soon as you start to explore you will meet a number of different sorts of commands, all carried out in a different way. These commands are consistent but sometimes will not seem that way to a new user.

(c) Advanced

WordCraft will take some time to learn and become familiar with but once you have cracked it you will have a powerful tool. WordCraft documents can be sent straight to a **typesetting** machine and if you purchase some of the add-ons it can become a **desk-top publisher**.

You can now create and manipulate up to 32 data columns or seven text columns, all of varying dimensions, newspaper or parallel style.

There is a *communications* link and *data conversion* is straightforward. The **mail box** is ideal for modern offices but does not replace a specially-designed communication program and you still need a modem. Files can be imported from and exported to WordStar.

Index and **table of contents** generation is supplied.

The **calculation** commands are highly sophisticated and include automatic recalculation and use of formulae.

There is a **tree** command to display the construction of directories.

Double underlining is now included and all fonts and pitches are named on the screen at the point where they are operational.

You can create any number of dictionaries, each of which can contain up to 100,000 words, and can use two dictionaries at once.

There is a **database** feature which will sort and select records and integrates with the **merge** facility.

The **macro** feature is called **phrase**.

(d) How it works

The WordCraft workscreen is split into *three sections*. The top of the screen tells you whether you are in **command mode** or **type mode**. Use the **Esc** key to **toggle** between the two modes. This section also tells you about the current position of the cursor and the logged directory/drive.

When you are in **command mode** the cursor will wait for you to key-in your command in this part of the screen. Perhaps you want to **get** a file or change the page **length**. To carry out many commands you just key-in the command you want and follow the onscreen instructions. However, you will probably need a manual to explain the instructions. Some of the **commands** can also be carried out by means of the *function keys*, these are displayed in the lower third of the screen. A full list of **commands** can be displayed at any time.

When you are in **type mode** the cursor will be below the command area, separated by the **ruler**. Text will wrap round the screen and text will insert to the left of the cursor.

A translation of the function keys runs along the base of the screen. These keys are **soft**, which means that when you press a key you may access another menu and all the translations will change. You may go down through the menus by selecting commands and may then need to return to the workscreen by the same route.

Additional commands are carried out by pressing the **Alt** key at the same time as a letter or number. Other commands use **Ctrl** with a cursor movement key and make cursor movement more efficient. However, the **Ctrl End** command is used to delete the current line. So you will find some oddities.

Start up

When the **A>** or **C>** is displayed key-in **loadw** and press **Enter**. While WordCraft loads into memory you may be asked to replace the system disk with another disk because some of the files are needed.

Create Document

As soon as the workscreen is displayed you are in **command mode**, so press **Esc** to be in **type mode**. You can now key-in your text. Default margins will be used but to change them position the cursor in the column where the margin is needed and use the **ruler** function key.

Insert

Text will insert automatically. Use the **Ins** key to **toggle** between **insert** and **overtype** modes.

Delete

Text can be deleted one character at a time, word by word, from the cursor to the end of the line, line by line, from the cursor to the end of the sentence or to the end of the page. You can also "zap" the entire document on the screen and clear it. There is an **undo delete** command too.

Pages

You can set the length of the text and also the length of the paper. A page break will be thrown automatically by the system when the text length is exceeded but you can also set your own page break as required. A new page always starts at the top of the screen.

Print

You can print the document currently displayed on the screen or another named file, by *specified page* or *chapter*.

Cut and Paste

You can copy and move blocks of text within the same document. To copy text from one document to another you are advised to put the text into a **phrase** and recall it in the target document.

INDEX